No More Independent Reading Without Support

DEAR READERS,

Much like the diet phenomenon *Eat This, Not That*, this series aims to replace some existing practices with approaches that are more effective—healthier, if you will—for our students. We hope to draw attention to practices that have little support in research or professional wisdom and offer alternatives that have greater support. Each text is collaboratively written by authors representing research and practice. Section 1 offers a practitioner's perspective on a practice in need of replacing and helps us understand the challenges, temptations, and misunderstandings that have led us to this ineffective approach. Section 2 provides a researcher's perspective on the lack of research to support the ineffective practice(s) and reviews research supporting better approaches. In Section 3, the authors representing a practitioner's perspective give detailed descriptions of how to implement these better practices. By the end of each book, you will understand both what not to do, and what to do, to improve student learning.

It takes courage to question one's own practice—to shift away from what you may have seen throughout your years in education and toward something new that you may have seen few if any colleagues use. We applaud you for demonstrating that courage and wish you the very best in your journey from this to that.

Best wishes,

—*Ellin Oliver Keene and Nell K. Duke, series editors*

No More Independent Reading Without Support

DEBBIE MILLER and BARBARA MOSS

HEINEMANN
Portsmouth, NH

Heinemann
361 Hanover Street
Portsmouth, NH 03801–3912
www.heinemann.com

Offices and agents throughout the world

The authors and publisher wish to thank those who have generously given permission to reprint borrowed material:

"Bureaucracy 3" from *The Book of Embraces* by Eduardo Galeano, translated by Cedric Belfrage with Mark Schafer. Copyright © 1989 by Eduardo Galeano. English translation copyright © 1991 by Cedric Belfrage. Reprinted by permission of the author and W. W. Norton & Company, Inc.

Acknowledgments for borrowed material continue on page viii.

Library of Congress Cataloging-in-Publication Data
Miller, Debbie.
    No more independent reading without support / Debbie Miller and Barbara Moss.
        pages cm
    Includes bibliographical references.
    ISBN 978-0-325-04904-5
    1. Reading. 2. Reading comprehension. 3. Children—Books and reading.
I. Title.

LB1573.M4937 2013
372.4—dc23   2013019675

Series editors: Nell K. Duke and Ellin Oliver Keene
Acquisitions editor: Margaret LaRaia
Production: Vicki Kasabian
Cover design: Lisa A. Fowler
Cover photograph: Getty Images/Westend61
Interior design: Suzanne Heiser
Typesetting: Valerie Levy, Drawing Board Studios
Manufacturing: Veronica Bennett

Printed in the United States of America on acid-free paper
17 16 15 14   VP   3 4 5

CONTENTS

SECTION 3 **BUT THAT**

An Instructional Framework for Supporting Classroom Independent Reading

Debbie Miller

INTRODUCTION

NELL K. DUKE

When districts around the country eliminated time for Drop Everything and Read (DEAR), Uninterrupted Sustained Silent Reading (USSR), and other independent reading periods in response to the National Reading Panel Report (National Institute of Child Health and Human Development 2000), I didn't know what to think. On the one hand, reading—a lot—is clearly essential to becoming a strong reader; if students who choose not to read at home aren't given time to read at school, when will they read? On the other hand, I'd sat through many hours of DEAR and USSR that seemed like at best a waste of time and at worst a surefire way to further turn students off reading. I even came to refer to DEAR as "Drop Everything and Find Waldo" as I watched students spend this valuable time searching for the stripe-hatted Waldo in the popular Where's Waldo? books—without ever reading a word.

Debbie Miller and Barbara Moss help us see how to do independent reading right—to live up to its promise as a means to support reading development and engagement. Moss updates us with some very important research that shows the positive impact independent reading periods in school can have if done well. Miller helps us see how to find time for independent reading and how to provide students with the kind of supports that will make independent reading effective.

It is a privilege to edit a book by these two renowned writers and thinkers. I expect that you will leave their book with a renewed sense of purpose and new strategies for fostering independent reading in your classroom. Now off we go; it's time to read.

Credit lines for borrowed material continued from the copyright page:

Figure 2–1: "What Is Scaffolded Silent Reading?" from "Exploring Scaffolded Silent Reading (ScSR): Effective Practice for Increasing Reading Fluency and Comprehension" by Ray Reutzel, Utah State University. http://reading.org/downloads/WC_handouts/Exploring%20Scaffolded%20Silent%20Reading%20(ScSR).pdf. Reprinted by permission of the author.

Excerpts from Common Core State Standards © Copyright 2010. National Governors Association Center for Best Practices and Council of Chief State School Officers. All rights reserved.

NOT THIS

Is There Enough Time? And Is Time Enough to Support Independent Reading?

DEBBIE MILLER

Finding the Time

Children learn to read by reading . . . but not without instructional support. It's well known that in order to become thoughtful, strategic, proficient readers, children need to read. A lot. When children read extensively, they learn about themselves, other people, and the world; they learn that reading is something they can do that empowers them to control their lives, connect with each other, and make the world a better place. For children to develop the habits and identity of thoughtful, strategic, proficient readers, they need to practice and, to make their practice productive, they need the tools that we can provide through

> For the evidence that independent reading is essential to student achievement
>
> see Section 2, pages 11–14

1

instruction. This extensive independent reading practice framed by instruction needs to happen in classrooms every day.

Maybe you're thinking, "I hear you. If I had more minutes in the day, I really would give independent reading time a try. But my day is jam-packed as it is—I can't imagine squeezing in one more thing." I get it—with all that's being asked of teachers and children, it's no wonder you might feel overwhelmed, out of sync, and just a little frantic.

But what if there were a way out? What if there were a way—at least for part of the day—where things slowed down, your students had their hands and minds on great books, and you had the pleasure of conferring with them about their reading and themselves as readers? No rotations, activities, or worksheets—just you, your kids, and books.

If you could find a way out, would you take it?

Eighteen brave teachers in a K–5 school just outside Baltimore did. I was scheduled for a three-day visit, and on the first two days I worked with children in classrooms, demonstrating in each a short focus lesson, thirty to sixty minutes of independent reading and conferring, and a reflection time where children reflected on their reading and what they'd learned about themselves as readers that day—the instructional framework I call "readers' workshop."

To learn the practices to support independent reading

see Section 3, pages 41–69, and the research that informs these practices in Section 2

Over a luscious crab cake dinner the night of day two (this was Baltimore after all!), teachers, their literacy coach, and principal had a "come to independent reading" moment. They realized they'd been doing all this stuff "about" reading, but kids never got to actually read and practice what teachers were working so hard to teach them. They had Drop Everything and Read (DEAR) time at the end of the day, but there was no instructional focus for this time—kids would grab a book and read until the timer sounded. And teachers just tried to keep them on task.

"We don't really know our children as readers," teachers reflected. "We've learned more about them in two days than we've learned about them all year," they told me. They explained that during DEAR time, teachers read, too. Because this was the only time children read independently, teachers weren't able to confer with children and find out about them as readers. "Plus," they told me, "we realize our children don't have anything specific to practice during DEAR time, and we're not even sure they're really reading. So yes. We're in! How do we get more time for independent reading?"

My answer? First, let's find the minutes. And then let's figure out how to use them well.

⊹⊹ ⊹ ⊹⊹ ⊹ ⊹⊹ ⊹ ⊹⊹

How Can You Find the Minutes?

In Eduardo Galleano's short story "Bureaucracy 3," he writes:

> At a barracks in Seville, in the middle of the courtyard of that barracks was a small bench. Next to the small bench, a soldier stood guard. No one knew why the bench had to be guarded. It was guarded around the clock—every day, every night, and from one generation of officers to the next, the order was passed on and the soldiers obeyed it. No one expressed any doubts or ever asked why. If that's how it was done, there had to be a reason.
>
> And so it continued until someone, some general or colonel, wanted to look at the original order. He had to rummage through all the files. After a good bit of poking around, he found the answer. Thirty-one years, two months and four days ago, an officer had ordered a guard to be stationed beside the small bench, which had just been painted, so that no one would think of sitting on wet paint. (1992, 64)

What Benches Are You Guarding?

If you're looking to find the time for independent reading during the school day, what benches/practices might you be guarding? Which ones do you believe must stay? Which ones might you modify or stop protecting altogether? Here's how my colleagues and friends in Baltimore worked through these questions.

To learn what happened when teachers evaluated their time

see Section 3, page 44

They asked me and their literacy coach to help them find the thirty to sixty minutes (depending on grade level) they needed every day for independent reading.

Here's a sampling of some of the actions and activities we noticed across the day and the grades that gave us all pause.

Calendar activities. Our first visit was kindergarten. Children were gathered in the meeting area doing calendar activities, dutifully filling in the blanks with their voices: "Today is _____. Yesterday was _____. Tomorrow will be _____." They found the day and date on the calendar, and sang the "There Are Seven Days in a Week" song. Next their teacher marked how many days they'd been in school on the number line, and children counted and clapped from one all the way to 106. They grouped the number of days they'd been in school by tens and ones using straws and rubber bands. And then they dressed the bear.

"What's the weather like outside?" their teacher asked. "How should we dress Paddy the Bear?" "It's cold and snowy!" the children chorused. So Paddy needed a coat with buttons. Paddy needed boots with buckles. And Paddy, even though he's covered in fur from head to toe (and staying inside), also needed a hat that tied. Dressing Paddy is hard work when you're just learning how to button and buckle and tie. Not to mention time-consuming.

Twenty-seven minutes later, we moved to grade 1. One glance at the whiteboard and I knew what they were up to. It was calendar time!

I saw the straws ready to be bundled and the number line ready to be counted, and I heard children singing, "There are seven days in a week and I know what their names are. . . ." And then I spied him. Paddy. Patiently waiting to be buttoned, buckled, and tied.

Would it surprise you that grade 2 had calendar activities that included Paddy too? I'm not against calendar activities—I've done all these things myself! But how much time, effort, and energy should they take? Over how many days and weeks and years? And do children need to dress a bear to figure out what to put on when they go outside to play? Might they already know?

What else did we notice?

Schoolwide morning announcements. These took up to ten minutes every day, what with announcing the day, the date, what happened on this day in history, reminders for after-school activities (tae kwon do in the gym, Scouts in room 207, jump rope practice in the lunchroom) and the upcoming food drive, book fair, and the candy/candle/wrapping paper sale. Next, birthdays were announced (birthday boys and girls trooped to the office for a Happy Birthday Pencil), the school song was sung, and a sweet-voiced child read the poem of the day.

Transitions. There was a lot of flicking of lights, and "Get quiet by the time I count to ten," "We can't go until everyone's cleaned up and ready," and "I'm waiting" kind of talk we found. Dozens of minutes a day devoted to moving from one subject to another, passing out papers, and other organizational details that took away from constructive learning time.

Lining up. In many classrooms lining up was quite the procedure. For example:

> "If you are wearing stripes, you may line up." (Then on to plaid, checks, etc.)

"If your name starts with *A*, you may line up." (Then on to *B, C, D*, etc.)

"If you are the line leader, you may invite a child to line up." (Then on to that child offering an invitation, and on and on and on.)

The reading block. Oh my goodness—this was an eye-opener for everyone! Across the grades children were doing a staggering number of things *about* reading (and math and handwriting and coloring, too) but very little actual reading. These included:

- worksheets and worksheet packets (As in the more you got done, the more there were, just ready and waiting for you. And these worksheets weren't limited to reading—they also included math, handwriting, and now and again a writing prompt.)
- test-prep materials (All. Year. Long.)
- looking up definitions of vocabulary words in the dictionary, writing them three times and using them in a sentence, and/or writing an entire story using all the words (Those were *some* stories!)
- reading, spelling, and math workbooks
- word searches and jumbles
- answering end-of-story comprehension questions from the basal reader
- centers (coloring, cutting and pasting, math activities, making paper plate and paper sack puppets, using a document camera to fill out a worksheet and project it on the wall)
- guided reading (There's nothing wrong with guided reading groups, but they shouldn't take over the entire reading block. In some instances, children did have opportunities to read independently during this time, but they had no opportunity to confer with their teacher—she was busy getting through three or four groups. In many classrooms, children rotated through centers during this time, and although some did include reading activities, there was little real reading.)

- completing accelerated reading tests or other computer programs, not to mention counting points for prizes
- endless browsing in an effort to find a "just-right" book
- schoolwide DEAR time, the last twenty minutes of the day, with children and teachers all reading during this time
- packing up to go home (In some classrooms, children started packing up and cleaning up a full fifteen minutes before the final bell.)

More Than Just DEAR or Sustained Silent Reading

Finding the time can feel like the biggest challenge to independent reading in the classroom, but time isn't the only thing we need to think about. When students sit quietly at their desk with a book or magazine during DEAR or Sustained Silent Reading (SSR) time, we might see them flip a page every minute or so, but we can't see what's happening inside their heads. We don't have evidence of how they're making meaning of

> **For the research that explains why students need more than time for independent reading**
>
> see Section 2, pages 11–13

the text, the specific ways they've grown as readers, or what they're struggling with as they read. Without that information, we can't teach them how to get better and we can't be sure that—even if they read every day—all students *are* becoming better readers this week than they were the one before.

SSR and DEAR appeal to so many teachers because they've been told that reading together creates community and that by reading a book while their students read, they're modeling what being a good reader looks like. But how much information is a student gathering from watching a teacher read? Not much. The student observes quiet eyes focused on the text for a set period of time, some page turning, perhaps a gasp or chuckle, but mostly nothing that couldn't be communicated by a photograph of someone reading. It's an intention that's on the right track, but misses the mark.

For students to do more than race through lots of books, they need a teacher to show them what behaviors they need to practice as they read, and the teacher needs opportunities to monitor and give feedback on how students are using those behaviors. With SSR and DEAR, both the students' and the teacher's process of making meaning of a text are invisible and can't influence one another. Teachers need to talk about how they make meaning of a text so that the process is "visible" to students. As students practice, the teacher monitors students' reading, through talk and writing, so that students get feedback that helps them get better. Sometimes the feedback helps students choose the right book, one that lets them experience some success. Unguided choice and lack of monitoring can mean that students see struggle while reading as their own permanent deficiency. If they don't understand when that struggle is part of the process of reading and growing as a reader, children come to accept that what they read won't make sense and that some people, like them, aren't really readers. Independent reading in silence without the kind of support described in this book means these children suffer in silence.

Just to be clear—children should have a number of opportunities to read throughout the day; some will be more structured than others. But when nonstructured scenarios are the *only* opportunities for children to read—when independent reading stands alone with no instructional framework, such as DEAR and SSR—it's simply not enough. When we "set children loose" day after day after day, with no focus or support, it can lead to fake reading and ultimately disengagement (as you'll see in Section 2), whether it's due to lack of purpose or a perceived or actual lack of reading skill. It's our job to do everything we can to equip children

How can you structure independent reading time in a way that is effective for all children?

see Section 3, pages 47–69

with the tools they need to stay engaged and motivated when we're not there, when they don't have a grown-up giving them the command to "drop everything and read."

The more opportunities we can give children to read, the better. My Baltimore friends understood that—they just couldn't find the time in their overcrowded day. For decades we have understood that providing long and growing periods of time for independent reading, along with focused instruction, is essential for children's growth as readers.

So now, let's look at what the research tells us about independent reading and why making it work for all children is so important.

SECTION 2

WHY NOT? WHAT WORKS?

Why Independent Reading Matters and the Best Practices to Support It

BARBARA MOSS

Does Independent Reading Influence Student Achievement?

You have probably heard independent reading (IR) called by one or more of these terms: *Sustained Silent Reading* (SSR), *Drop Everything and Read* (DEAR), *Uninterrupted Sustained Silent Reading* (USSR), *individualized reading, recreational reading, voluntary reading,* and most recently *independent reading.* You might also have thought of programs like Accelerated Reader™ or Scholastic Reading Counts!,™ where students read books and take online quizzes to earn points. These different understandings of IR call for a clear definition, so here's a simple one: IR refers to time students spend reading self-selected texts (adapted from Gambrell et al. 2011). Whether in school, out of school, or both, children reading on their own is an established educational practice and, as we'll see, experimental studies prove it can be an effective one. This section will show you that IR is an essential practice, one that develops

> **Can time spent reading independently in school translate to academic performance? Yes.**
>
> It can:
>
> • improve students' oral reading accuracy
>
> • increase reading rate
>
> • improve reading expression
>
> • increase reading comprehension
>
> if teachers scaffold IR by
>
> • modeling and teaching students to self-select books from a variety of genres at their IR levels
>
> • confer with students
>
> • monitor and provide feedback to students
>
> • make students accountable for their reading

(Reutzel, Fawson, and Smith 2008)

background knowledge, improves fluency and comprehension, heightens motivation, increases reading achievement, and helps students broaden their vocabulary.

Despite this, many schools have dropped or decreased their attention to IR in favor of literacy instruction that they believe will raise test scores. Ironically, they've eliminated one of the most powerful ways to improve student achievement. In one study of fifth graders, for example, those who spent time reading books outside of school achieved better on standardized tests than kids who didn't (Anderson, Wilson, and Fielding 1988). Students who read independently an hour a day scored at the 98th percentile on standardized tests, while students who read only 4.6 minutes daily scored at the 50th percentile, and students who did no out-of-school reading scored at the 2nd percentile. Although the study did not definitely prove that reading outside of school caused the increased achievement, it did establish a relationship between IR and academic achievement.

Later studies, such as Reutzel, Fawson, and Smith (2008), have demonstrated the contribution IR makes to academic achievement. In response to questions of the effectiveness of SSR in isolation, Reutzel and colleagues tested a structured form of in-school IR called *Scaffolded Silent Reading* (ScSR). See Figure 2–1.

The study found that in-school IR led to gains that were better than national averages in reading rates and a 43 percent average increase in the proportion of ideas recalled, representing a substantial increase in comprehension over the school year.

And yet, despite the evidence, IR is a neglected practice: students don't read much outside of school; only one third of thirteen-year-olds read on a daily basis (National Endowment for the Arts 2007), and most students do little IR in their classrooms (National Center for Education Statistics 2011).

If We Know Independent Reading Is Effective, Why Don't We Do It?

Why has IR faded from the classroom scene in recent years? Teachers give lots of reasons for not doing IR, citing scarce instructional time, students who aren't ready for reading on their own, or the difficulty of managing IR with a wide range of levels in classrooms. In addition, the *Report of the National Reading Panel* (NRP; National Institute of Child Health and Human Development 2000) appeared dismissive of the practice when they said that insufficient *experimental* research exists to support IR: "Literally hundreds of correlational studies find that the best readers read the most and that poor readers read the least. Many correlational studies tell us that the more children read, the better their comprehension, vocabulary, and fluency. However, these findings are correlational in nature and correlation does not imply causation" (3).

What does this mean? When we talk about correlation, we mean that there is a statistical relationship between two variables. For example, researchers have found correlations between attractiveness and job success, but this does not mean that attractiveness *causes* job success.

Figure 2-1 What is scaffolded silent reading?

Key Characteristics	Traditionally Implemented SSR	ScSR
Teacher instructional role	Model for students silent reading of self-selected books.	Teach and scaffold students' appropriate book selection strategies.
Classroom library or book collection design	Books are stored and displayed in variant ways across classroom contexts.	A variety of genres are stored and displayed within designated levels of reading difficulty.
Characteristics of reading motivation/ engagement	Student free choice of reading materials is encouraged.	Student choice is circumscribed to encourage wide reading using a genre selection wheel.
Level of text difficulty	Students freely choose the level of difficulty of reading materials.	Students choose texts at their IR levels with teacher support.
Teaching monitoring and feedback	None	Teacher initiates brief (five-minute) individual student reading conferences.
Student accountability	None	Students read aloud to the teacher, answer teacher questions, set personal goals for completing the reading of a book within a time frame, and complete one or more book response projects.

Adapted from Reutzel et al. (2008, 197)

Clearly, there are many other variables contributing to workplace success. In other words, the NRP found there were many correlational studies showing a relationship between IR and achievement, but there weren't enough experimental studies to prove that IR *caused* improved achievement. In experimental studies, researchers typically compare approaches using a control group and experimental group and control for variables that affect study results. It is through these kinds of studies that we can more confidently say that a practice like IR *causes* improved achievement.

The fact that the NRP did not endorse IR might have contributed to the decline of this practice within the school day, prompting schools to abandon IR for other approaches. However, since the publication of the NRP report, a new generation of experimental studies demonstrated that IR can promote achievement gains under specific conditions that we will discuss in this section. These studies fill the gap in the research noted by the NRP, creating a new body of knowledge around this topic and igniting increased enthusiasm for this practice.

A New Reason for Independent Reading: The Common Core State Standards

The Common Core State Standards for English Language Arts and Literacy in History/Social Studies Science and Technical Subjects (National Governors Association Center for Best Practices 2010) explicitly call for IR. Reading anchor standard number 10 lays out the expectation that students will "read and comprehend complex literary and informational texts independently and proficiently" (National Governors Association Center for Best Practices 2010, 10). While this standard does not explicitly state that IR must occur during the school day, it does make IR a requirement at all grade levels. Furthermore, it specifies *what* students should be reading—complex texts from a variety of genre. The standards argue that current practices have not done enough to foster *independent* reading of complex texts, especially informational texts (see page 3, Appendix A). In the "Revised Publishers Criteria for the Common Core State Standards" (Coleman and Pimentel 2012), the authors state that students should have "daily opportunities to read texts of their choice on their own during and outside of the school day. Students should have access to a wide range of materials on a variety of topics and genres . . . including informational texts and literary nonfiction as well as literature" (6–7).

For the details on how to translate these principles into classroom practice

see Section 3, page 47

What Practices Are Critical for Effective Independent Reading?

For students to achieve the skill levels we hope for, their IR needs to be supported by a collection of effective practices. Student growth happens when the following practices exist together.

To grow as independent readers, students need
• Classroom time to read
• To choose what they read
• Explicit instruction about what, why, and how readers read
• To read a lot: a large number of books and variety of texts
• Access to texts
• Teacher monitoring, assessment, and support during IR
• To talk about what they read

Students Need to Be Given Classroom Time to Read

If our goal is for students to read independently, then we have to make it a practice that happens during classroom time. As the Baltimore teachers shared in Section 1, it can seem difficult to find time for IR, but the research tells us that it's time well spent. In a study of 1,285 first and second graders and their 107 teachers, Foorman et al. (2006) identified twenty ways students spend instructional time including oral language, grammar, vocabulary, letter recognition, and word work and text reading. They used these to predict students' end-of-year reading achievement scores. The *only* variable that explained gains on the posttest was time spent on actual text reading; time spent on other factors like phonemic awareness, word, or alphabetic instruction failed to predict improved achievement. This does not mean that phonemic awareness and word and alphabetic instruction is not important, but that the extent to which it occurred was not what separated the more successful classes from the less successful ones. In two studies of effective teaching, one of the indicators of effective teaching was time spent on IR, with less effective teachers' students spending more time on worksheets, answering literal questions, or completing activities (Allington 2002; Taylor et al. 2003). In a study of uses of student time in successful reading interventions, two-thirds of student time was spent reading and rereading (Allington 2011). So, we know students should be reading independently during classroom time, but how much time is enough?

The "Just-Right" Amount of Independent Reading Time May Depend on Reader Proficiency.

There is no clear-cut answer to the question of how much IR is optimal. Typically teachers allocate about twenty minutes for IR (Lewis and Samuels 2005), but the answer may well depend upon the reader's proficiency. In a study comparing two similar groups that were not

> For some practical advice on helping kids develop reading stamina
>
> see Section 3, pages 57, 61

randomly assigned (Wu and Samuels 2004), fifteen minutes was compared to forty minutes of daily IR in grades 3–5. All students read books matched to their ability and were quizzed on their reading. Results of the study were mixed. Poor readers gained more in word recognition and vocabulary than good readers, while good readers made gains in speed and comprehension. Good readers benefited more from the forty-minute IR time on all measures than poor readers, but poor readers gained more on all measures from the fifteen additional reading minutes than better readers did. The authors concluded that students with different reading abilities have different achievement patterns based on the amount of time they spend in reading independently. In this study, fifteen minutes of reading time for low readers "appears to be more beneficial than 40 minutes for improving skills such as reading speed and comprehension" (19), perhaps because they haven't yet developed stamina for reading over longer periods of time. What this study suggests is that different time allocations should be provided for students at different stages of development. In her meta-analysis of dozens of studies of IR, Lewis (2002) concluded that, "Time is an obvious factor in learning. . . . However, the amount of time must be adequate to meet the demands of the task or the needs of the student" (179). Clearly, more research is needed on this topic, specifically exploring how students may do if they are given longer periods of time over the course of the school year.

Students Need to Be Able to Choose What They Read

For advice on how to support choice

see Section 3, page 50

Within that time set aside for IR, what should kids be reading? The research says that IR is most effective when students choose their own reading materials. According to Allington and Gabriel (2012), "The research base on student selected reading is robust and conclusive. Students read more, understand more, and are more likely to continue reading when they have the opportunity to choose what they read" (10).

Why is choice so important? Think about your own reading habits. When you find time to read materials that are not school- or work-related, you probably pick topics that interest you. Like most people, I do lots of "required reading" in connection with my work as a professor. When not reading for professional purposes, I choose to read about topics very different from work reading. My tastes run toward lighter fare—reading the newspaper, historical fiction, books about travel, and the occasional guilty pleasure of *People* magazine!

Our students are like this too. Much of their reading in school is from required texts. It is important that we balance school reading opportunities with choice reading experiences. Kids who read self- rather than teacher-selected books read more (Reynolds and Symons 2001), and self-selected reading is twice as powerful as teacher-selected reading in developing motivation and comprehension (Guthrie and Humenick 2004; Lindsay 2010). Letting kids choose what to read motivates them to read even when it is not required (Ainley, Hidi, and Berndorff 2002) and gives students practice in selecting their own books, which can contribute to out-of-school reading (Ivey and Broaddus 2001; Reis et al. 2008). So, if we want students to read outside the classroom, then we need IR in the classroom to be centered around student-selected texts.

Students Need Explicit Instruction About What, Why, and How Readers Read

As part of earlier classroom IR practices like SSR and DEAR, children selected books with little teacher oversight. This practice was especially problematic because poor readers often picked books that they couldn't read (Anderson 2009; Donovan, Smolkin, and Lomax 2000). This finding will come as no surprise to most of you!

For examples of what explicit instruction can look like

see Section 3, page 51

Newer studies have established that productive student IR experiences depend on teachers who help students identify appropriate, interesting materials, incorporating a range of genres and difficulty levels (Reutzel et al. 2008; Trudel 2007). As part of their research on ScSR (Reutzel, Jones, Fawson, and Smith 2008; Reutzel et al. 2008), the authors taught teachers how to model book selection strategies that included picking books of appropriate difficulty, locating those books in the classroom

For other tools students can use to be aware of genre and to ensure they read widely

see Section 3, page 52

library, selecting books from different genre, and recording their choices on a genre wheel. For one example of a genre wheel, see Figure 2–2.

This explicit teaching of book selection strategies is an essential aspect of classroom IR. Remember Debbie's comment in Section 1 about the time lost to students' endless browsing for book selection? Teachers who guide book selection facilitate time on task for all students (Block and Pressley 2007; Ehri et al. 2007) including struggling primary-level readers (Bryan, Fawson, and Reutzel 2003; Kamil 2008; Reutzel et al. 2008).

Figure 2–2 Genre Wheel

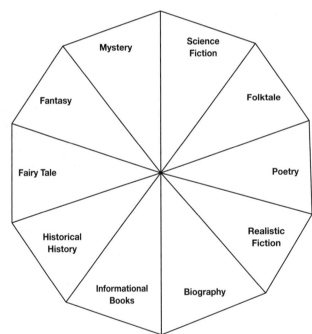

Direction to students: Read at least one book from all ten genres. When you've read a book, record the title in the correct genre and color it in.

How difficult should independent reading materials be? Traditionally, in IR children read easy materials. The "easiness" of a text is usually defined by students' word accuracy levels. Students know 98–99 percent of words in easy or independent-level texts, instructional or "just-right" level texts are those at 95–97 percent accuracy levels, and texts where accuracy falls below 95 percent are considered frustration level or difficult texts (Betts 1946). For IR, struggling readers may need a diet of successful reading experiences in books they can read with 99 percent accuracy or more (Allington 2009; Torgensen and Hudson 2006; Hiebert and Fisher 2012). For example, Ehri et al. (2007) found that when language-minority first graders practiced rereading previously read books, instructional-level book reading (90–97 percent accuracy in this study) did not promote reading growth, whereas reading independent-level (98–100 percent accuracy in this study) books did positively correlate with reading growth. Other studies have concluded that reading easier texts during IR resulted in achievement gains (Torgensen and Hudson 2006; Hiebert and Fisher 2012).

However, some research suggests that teachers need to monitor IR choices to ensure enough challenge to foster an individual reader's growth. In Carver and Liebert's (1995) study of summer reading, forty-three third, fourth, and fifth graders read easy self-selected books (at one or two grade levels below their reading level) two hours a day for six weeks. This combined sixty hours of reading time did not result in improved reading achievement, vocabulary, or improved rate. The authors argued that letting students read only easy materials contributed to a lack of reading progress. Reading harder texts may benefit rather than harm student achievement and help students grow as readers (Kuhn and Stahl 2000; Kuhn and Schwanenflugel 2009; O'Conner et al. 2002) and reading books that are too easy over time may hamper growth (Baker and Wigfield 1999).

Children can successfully negotiate harder books if appropriate teacher scaffolding is provided. In an IR enrichment intervention with students in grades 3–5 (Reis et al. 2008), students in the experimental group received one hour of basal reader instruction and one hour of IR while the control group received two hours of basal instruction. Students in the experimental group were coached by their teachers to select high-interest books slightly above their current reading levels and showed statistically significant gains over the control group. In a study that looked at IR accompanied by coaching, students successfully engaged in independent fluency practice with materials in which they had only 85 percent word accuracy. The authors argued that the level of text difficulty for fluency practice is inversely related to the amount of student scaffolding provided (Stahl and Heuback 2005). If we want students to grow, it seems logical to provide them with the right degree of challenge and support in facing that challenge, and there will undoubtedly be more studies exploring this important question. Based on the available research (more is certainly needed), it seems that either approach—coaching students toward selecting independent-level texts or coaching students toward selecting more difficult texts—is defensible. Perhaps most advisable at this point is encouraging engagement with texts of varying levels of difficulty, providing greater support for students when they select more difficult texts. In addition, the word reading level and comprehension level of a given student do not always align (e.g., Halladay 2012; Buly and Valencia 2002). A text that may appear independent for the student in terms of word reading may actually be too difficult for the student in terms of comprehension and vice versa. All of these findings suggest the need to be responsive, rather than dogmatic, regarding reading levels during IR.

For some details on genre-specific reading instruction

see Section 3, page 52

Students need genre-specific reading instruction. When researchers call for direct, explicit instruction to support IR, they refer to a wide range of skills, not only teaching students how to pick a book that's interesting and at an appropriate level of difficulty but also how to read strategically from books in different genres, how to engage in book discussions, how to overcome difficulties in texts, and how to think more deeply about texts. Explicit instruction can happen in large- or small-group lessons or during one-to-one conversations between a teacher and student—but it needs to happen early in children's schooling so that students get lots of practice. One neglected area of explicit instruction is genre-specific reading instruction.

Think about the reading you do in a given day as a teacher—you may read a newspaper, email messages, your students' science text, notes from parents, online interviews, novels, or an interview with an author. We read on- and off-line, we read information, we read stories, and much more. In the real world, we encounter a multiplicity of text types or genre. For students to fully reap the benefits of IR, teachers need to show students how to read a variety of texts. Each genre has unique features and reading comprehension is genre-dependent (Duke and Roberts 2010). Genre-specific strategies such as attending to character, setting, problem, and resolution when reading narrative text and reading for main ideas with informational text facilitate student understanding of specific text types. In other words, the reading processes used to comprehend a story like *Charlotte's Web* are different from those needed to extract information from an article on spiders. Furthermore, those processes used for reading online and off-line are also different (Coiro and Dobler 2007). Simply teaching comprehension generically may not be effective; students need explicit instruction in specific strategies unique to reading and writing in particular genre if they are to successfully negotiate the many text types they should encounter as part of IR. Conferring during IR should not sound the same regardless of what students are reading. Rather, the type of text the student is reading should influence the specific strategies the teacher encourages the student to use. For example, a student reading a mystery might be encouraged to make lots of predictions about "who done it" along the way, whereas a student reading an encyclopedia might be helped to use the index to find information on topics of greatest interest.

Boost the Number of Texts Students Read

To become readers who can master the complex texts necessary for college and workplace success, students need to read a lot. This goal, stated in the Common Core State Standards, did not come out of thin air but was informed by the work of researchers like Adams (2009) who explains that "there may one day be modes and methods of information delivery that are as efficient and powerful as text, but for now there is no contest. To grow, our students must read lots, and more specifically they must read lots of 'complex' texts—texts that offer them new language, new knowledge, and new modes of thought" (182).

By increasing reading volume, students can improve reading achievement. Guthrie, Schafer, and Huang (2001) found that students who scored proficient and advanced on the National Assessment of Educational Progress (NAEP) read *twice as many words in school* than students at the below basic level. On the 2009 NAEP, children who reported reading for fun almost every day had higher average scores than those who read less often (National Center for Education Statistics 2009). One of the dangers in emphasizing reading volume is that it can lead to some mistaken practices, like reading competitions. The number of books or pages read is not the goal and focusing on that can mean that students skim books rather than read deeply. What we mean by volume is that reading becomes a daily habit.

Volume matters. My hair stylist recently used "volumizing" shampoo on my hair. My limp, thin, weak hair was transformed: it appeared thick, luxurious, and full of body. In the same way, reading volume can create full-bodied readers, children who read a great variety and number of texts. While we can't inject each child with a volumizer, we can give them lots of reading practice over time, which increases their stamina for reading (Allington 2009). Children need the chance to practice reading every day, not just when their work is finished.

Core reading programs don't provide that "volumizing" boost that students, especially poorer readers, need. In many schools throughout the country, which may include your school, teachers are required to use core basal reading programs, often with "fidelity" (i.e., they can't deviate from the materials provided in the program). While schools, administrators, and teachers might find it tempting to rely exclusively on core reading programs to give students reading practice, these textbooks alone may not be enough to get children on the road to reading. Gamse et al. (2008) found that students made few gains in comprehension when basal reader content represented the primary type of text students encounter. Furthermore, textbooks often don't give children, especially struggling readers, practice in materials they can successfully read.

Brenner, Hiebert, and Tompkins (2009) asked the question: How much reading practice would students get in six third-grade core reading programs if their teacher followed the guidelines in the teachers' editions? The answer was: not very much. The mean volume of reading connected texts recommended in these programs was only fifteen minutes a day, just 17 percent of the time allocated to a typical ninety-minute reading/language arts block. Other studies confirm that the amounts of reading students do in school are limited (Donahue et al. 2001; Gambrell 1984; Foertsch 1992; Duke 2000a). Surveys of fourth graders in the 2011 NAEP (National Center for Education Statistics 2011) found that 38 percent of students read ten pages or less of text in school or for homework, which equals about eight to twelve minutes of daily reading (Brenner, Hiebert, and Tompkins 2009). If you are working in a school that uses a basal or core reading program, it is essential to provide additional time and materials for IR.

Students need experience reading a variety of texts. According to Palincsar and Duke (2004), literacy knowledge develops from literacy experiences. In other words, if we want students to read and comprehend lots of text types, they need experiences with different kinds of texts. We know that increasing the range and variety of texts increases reading competencies (Kuhn and Stahl 2000) and improves achievement not only in reading but other content areas (Guthrie et al. 2000). And when students were provided with a wide range of interesting books, effects on comprehension and motivation were substantial (Guthrie and Humenick 2004).

Because informational texts comprise the majority of adult professional reading, students need to spend time reading real-world informational texts. But most kids get minimal exposure to informational genres in school. Basal readers expose students to a narrow range of informational text types (Moss 2008), and children in preschool through third grade seldom hear informational texts read aloud whether at home or at school (Yopp and Yopp 2006). The picture in grades 2, 3, and 4 is equally bleak. In a study of second through fourth grader's experiences with informational texts, second graders experienced one minute per day of exposure to this text type, while third and fourth graders averaged only sixteen minutes per day (Jeong, Gaffney, and Choi 2010). This may, however, be changing. Results of a survey of 318 K–5 teachers found that teachers reported using informational text an average of thirty-two minutes a day, but this study unlike the others was self-reported data rather than observational. In any case, only about one-third of the books in classroom libraries were comprised of informational text (Ness 2011).

Another good reason to use informational text is that some children prefer informational texts to narratives (Kletzien and Szabo 1998; Cervetti et al. 2009; Caswell and Duke 1998). Brandon was one of these children. I met him during a school visit in Canton, Ohio. Brandon was passionate about animals. According to his teacher, most of the books he read in and out of school were informational books about this topic. I asked him about his interest in books about "real" topics. He clutched a book entitled *Rainforest Animals* (Savage 2006). He explained his fascination with facts with great seriousness: "I like information. Stories just tell you something silly like bears with clothes on. This gives more information than stories. It makes you smarter. Everything you think about is in this book" (Moss 2003, 37).

Fortunately for Brandon, his classroom was full of informational books. His teacher recognized his passion for facts and provided him with a steady stream of books that fueled that passion. If we want children to become lifelong readers, we need to give them materials that interest them, and to do so means including informational texts, historical fiction, poetry, magazines, graphic novels, and other genre.

Students Need Access to Texts

For children to find things they want to read, they need access to lots of materials; they need actual texts in their hands. According to Gambrell (1995), 90 percent of students get books from the school library. In a study of California school libraries, a statistically significant correlation was

For ideas on how to get books into kid's hands

see Section 3, page 55

found between the presence of a school library and standardized test achievement at the elementary and middle school levels (Sinclair-Tarr and Tarr 2007). The number of books in the library also matters. Krashen (1995) and McQuillan (1998) found that the number of books per student in the school library correlated with student test scores on the reading comprehension section of the NAEP for forty-one states.

The importance of libraries also extends to international comparisons. Elley (1992) looked at reading achievement of children in thirty-two countries and found that high-scoring countries (1) had large school and classroom libraries and (2) provided students with greater access to books at home, in community libraries, and in school. In another study, Krashen, Lee, and McQuillan (2012) found that access to books in school and public libraries was a significant predictor of fourth graders' reading scores on both the 2007 NAEP (Lee, Grigg, and Donahue 2007) and on the 2006 PIRLS (Progress in International Reading Literacy Study; Mullis et al. 2007), an international reading assessment of fourth graders in fourteen countries.

Experimental studies also support the importance of student access to books. Allington et al. (2010) studied 1,330 first- and second-grade low-income children's summer reading behaviors over a three-year period. Children were randomly assigned to a control group that received no books or a treatment group in which each child received twelve books for each of the three summers. Children self-selected titles from a book fair with many choices. Results of the intervention indicated a statistically significant improvement in student reading skills, particularly for children at lower-socioeconomic levels. The authors of this study explain their research and the practices that prevent summer reading loss in *No More Summer-Reading Loss* (Cahill et al. 2013).

Kim and White (2008) studied book access and not only matched children with books based on difficulty and interest, but also included scaffolded support from teachers. Third, fourth, and fifth graders from schools with populations that were primarily African American, Hispanic, and Asian participated in the study. Children were randomly assigned to the following groups: (1) a control group with no books, (2) a group that was given eight books during the summer, (3) a group that received eight books in the summer along with fluency lessons near the end of the school year, and (4) a group that got eight books along with fluency and comprehension lessons near the end of the school year. Results of the study found that those children who received both matched books and fluency and comprehension lessons made significantly greater gains from spring to fall.

Classroom libraries are essential. Children read 50 to 60 percent more in classrooms with libraries than without them (Morrow 2003; Neuman 1999; Kim 2003). The number of books in classrooms also seems to make a difference. In a study of thirty-two Maryland schools, Guthrie et al. (2000) surveyed 545 teachers to identify characteristics of schools that were improving over time in terms of reading achievement. They found that an abundance of trade books in classrooms predicted gains on statewide reading, writing, and science tests.

Clearly, access to books is not the same for all children, even if they have classroom and school libraries. Socioeconomic status dramatically impacts access (Neuman and Celano 2001; Duke 2000a; Neuman 1999; Duke 2000b). High-income students have access to four thousand times the number of books of low-income students (Neuman 1999). In comparing classroom libraries in low- and high-socioeconomic classrooms, Duke (2000a) found there were on average almost 40 percent fewer books and magazines in the low-socioeconomic classroom libraries when compared with high-socioeconomic classrooms. Poorer children depend on schools for books and reading materials because they often do not have books at home or bookstores in their neighborhoods (Neuman and Celano 2001). Unfortunately, these are the students who attend schools with poor school libraries (Constantino 2005; Constantino and Krashen 2008). Access to books for striving readers is especially important, since children at lower reading levels tend to read less and do more work-sheets, while those at higher levels tend to get more reading choices and greater exposure to expository texts (Chorzempa and Graham 2006). Krashen (2011) also identifies access to books as a factor in increased reading performance, while the evidence for workbooks, computer pro-grams, and other materials is not as strong (Dynarski et al. 2007). Unfor-tunately, Martinez et al. (1997) found that the proportion of lower-level books in classroom libraries was smaller than the need for such titles. The research strongly suggests, therefore, that districts, schools, and teachers should make providing access to large numbers of books a top priority.

So how many and what kinds of materials should you have in your library? Fountas and Pinnell (1996) recommend that teachers have between three hundred and six hundred titles in their classroom libraries. The International Reading Association (1999) recommends seven books per student. More importantly, you need materials that address top-ics that kids want to read about. In a classic study called "What Johnny Likes to Read Is Hard to Find in School," Worthy, Moorman, and Turner (1999) explored sixth graders' reading preferences. These kids wanted to read scary stories, comics and cartoons, and magazines and books about popular culture and sports, most of which they found outside of school. They ranked classrooms *last* as a source of interesting reading materi-als! The three-year study of the influence of summer book access refer-enced earlier arrived at a similar conclusion. Across three grade levels, 852 low-income students picked the same twelve or similar books from over four hundred book fair choices. Children were most interested in biographies of singers and actresses, Captain Underpants books, and other titles with popular culture and media tie-ins. The *least* popular titles included culturally relevant and curriculum-related titles (Allington et al. 2010). See Figure 2–3 for guidelines on creating a classroom library.

Students Need Teacher Monitoring, Assessment, and Ongoing Support During Independent Reading

During SSR and/or DEAR time in classrooms, students self-selected books, read for a specified time period, and did not typically respond to their reading in a specific way. With this model, teachers read self-selected materials during this time, with the intention of acting as a reading model for students. Sometimes teachers conferred with stu-

Figure 2–3   Guidelines for Creating Classroom Libraries

Recommended Number of Titles in Classroom Library

> 7 books per student (International Reading Association 1999)
> 300–600 books total (Fountas and Pinnell 1996)

Genres

> 50 percent literary
> 50 percent informational

Text Levels

> easy texts
> grade-level texts
> complex, or "stretch" texts

Text Types

comics	fantasy	biographies
magazines	poetry	realistic fiction
pop-culture titles	graphic novels	informational texts

---

dents or students shared their reading in some way, but these models typically were fairly unstructured in format. With SSR, the teacher was a participant in reading, rather than a facilitator of student learning. While more supportive of achievement than grading papers (Methe and Hinze 2003), having teachers read during IR is not motivating to children (Newman 2007), represents a passive instructional model, and does not increase student engagement (Widdowson, Dixon, and Moore 2006).

Newer evidence-based IR models require active teacher involvement during IR (Kelly and Clausen-Grace 2006; Reutzel et al. 2008; Fountas and Pinnell 2001; Reis et al. 2008). One of the biggest teacher concerns about IR I have heard relates to engaged reading time, or the amount of time when students are actively engaged with their eyes on the text. As Sarah, a teacher in my literacy master's degree program told me, "During whole-class instruction or guided reading, I can easily monitor student engagement. During IR, everyone is reading something different and kids get off task. It is hard to tell whether or not they are really reading and getting anything from their book choices. I've got thirty kids in thirty different books reading for thirty minutes, and sometimes I feel like the time provided for IR is time wasted. What can I do to make this time worthwhile for my students?"

The research suggests some specific practices that answer Sarah's question. A study by Block et al. (2009) compared five different approaches to silent IR to see what would happen to student reading comprehension scores if they gave 660 students in grades 2–6 twenty minutes of additional literacy instruction. Students in the control group got additional traditional basal reader instruction by reading stories and completing paper-and-pencil tasks. The experimental groups got one of these five treatments:

- *Independent silent skill practice*: Students read workbook passages.
- *Individual schema-based learning*: Students connected new learning to what they already knew. As students engaged in IR, teachers provided individualized instruction when students encountered obstacles.

- *Situated practice*: Teachers provided explicit strategy instruction and students silently practiced the strategy.
- *Conceptual learning*: Students self-selected, with teacher coaching, two expository trade books on the same topic and then read them back to back.
- *Transactional learning*: Readers silently read teacher-selected fiction books related to a thematic unit and engaged in teacher-monitored classroom discussions based on the texts.

At every grade level for all ability groups, individual schema-based learning, conceptual learning, and transactional learning produced the highest comprehension scores. Situated practice, workbook practice, and basal reader groups produced the lowest scores.

The authors concluded that if additional time is to be added to the daily reading diet, it should involve specific forms of teacher monitoring. The three most successful approaches included teacher monitoring of silent reading with personalized scaffolding of comprehension strategies. Successful teacher intervention behaviors included (1) teacher responding to student questions, (2) teacher-led discussions, and (3) teacher monitoring and modeling of comprehension strategies. According to the authors, "It is the specific actions that teachers take to support students during silent reading periods that produce significant growth in students' comprehension" (Block et al. 2009, 278). Figure 2–4 summarizes the actions teachers need to take to support students during IR, based on the studies outlined in this section.

Even disengaged readers stay on task when teachers support students during IR. Ways of supporting students can include launching students' reading with a demonstration of a fluency or comprehension strategy, letting students read self-selected books independently, and then monitoring students' reading through brief, teacher-initiated individual student conferences. During these conferences students read aloud from their book for one or two minutes so that the teacher

Figure 2–4 What teacher behaviors lead to student success during IR?

What teacher behaviors lead to student success during IR?

- Explicit lessons on how to select books at appropriate levels

- Explicit instruction on and teacher modeling of reading strategies that can be used during silent reading through shared reading and other methods

- Feedback on students' reading, whether oral or silent

- Reading conferences where students read aloud while teachers took running records, discussed books with the children, and set goals for future reading

- Student accountability for reading through postreading response activities including creation of posters, graphic organizers, written reactions, maintaining reading logs, maintaining reader response notebooks

- Large- and small-group discussion around the texts students read

can evaluate fluency, retell the text, and answer questions posed by the teacher. In addition, the student sets goals for text completion and chooses how she will respond to the text when finished reading (Bryan, Fawson, and Reutzel 2003). When students are engaged in their reading, they can read for longer periods of time, read through more difficult texts, and increase their reading achievement (Chow and Chou 2000; Guthrie 2004; Guthrie, Wigfield, and Perencevich 2004; McIntyre et al. 2006). Time spent reading without teacher guidance has a limited effect on achievement (Hansen et al. 2009; Topping, Samuels, and Paul 2007) and may be detrimental for striving readers (Reutzel et al. 2008). As one study explained: "Traditional procedures that provide time for reading without adequate preparation and scaffolds are unlikely to be associated with the benefits struggling readers require" (Hairrell et al. 2010, 275).

Want some practical advice on how to make conferring work for your student?

see Section 3, page 59

Differentiate instruction and create accountability through conferring. Making students accountable for reading can heighten student's active reading engagement (Reutzel, Jones, and Newman 2010). Conferring during IR time can be a meaningful way to make students accountable, provide individual help and guidance, and assess reading progress. Conferring is a challenge for many teachers who find it difficult to meet with students frequently enough to track progress. As a beginning teacher, I tried to implement conferring as part of twice weekly IR in a middle school setting. I had thirty-five students in each fifty-minute language arts class. Despite my best efforts, I found it nearly impossible to confer with more than about two students during each thirty-minute IR period. I finally gave up in frustration. I shouldn't have. There are ways to make conferring work.

Conferring research suggests that I was on the right track—IR is more effective when teachers confer with students (Garan and DeVoogd 2008; Manning and Manning 1984; Reis et al. 2008), and even brief conferences can be valuable. As part of the ScSR model (Reutzel, Fawson, and Smith 2008), teachers met with four to five students two to three times a week. You'll learn how to confer with larger numbers of students each week in Section 3.

Reis et al. (2008) found that individual, differentiated conferring resulted in higher student fluency scores. During these conferences, teachers assessed the match between student self-selected books and students' abilities by listening to them read, coaching students in using reading strategies, and engaging them in book discussions.

Provide supports for early readers. Early readers need more than teacher scaffolding for successful IR experiences. For these children, IR should include oral reading activities, not just silent reading. These nonsilent IR activities can include repeated reading, choral or echo reading, partner reading, or assisted oral reading (Brenner and Hiebert 2010; McIntyre et al. 2006) and should be balanced with explicit instruction in how to read. For example, strategies like the wide Fluency Oriented Reading Instruction (FORI) advocated by Kuhn and Schwanenflugel (2009) engaged students in scaffolded learning experiences where children read three different grade-level texts in a week. Children were introduced to texts through teacher-directed and shared reading experiences and practiced reading them through echo, partner, and choral reading. Students experienced both silent and oral reading through this approach, since they read silently as their partners read aloud.

Students Need to Talk About What They Read

Having students respond to their IR creates time for them to reflect on what they have read and to push their thinking further by sharing those reflections with others. Peer discussion is one way that students can demonstrate their knowledge of their reading, which helps to make them accountable and improves comprehension. Based upon their meta-analysis of forty-two empirical studies on classroom discussions and their effects on student comprehension and learning, Murphy et al. (2009) found that a number of discussion-based approaches including Instructional Conversations (Saunders and Goldenberg 1999) and Questioning the Author (Beck et al. 1997) contributed to student comprehension of text. Instructional Conversations are small-group discussions where the teacher prompts students' thinking by connecting their personal knowledge to the text. In these conversations, the teacher assumes the student has knowledge, skills, and values that will help expand the group's understanding of the text. Questioning the Author is a strategy that gives students authority as readers by letting them identify and evaluate how the author communicates ideas through text. These kinds of conversations benefit both fluent and limited English speakers (Saunders and Goldenberg 1999). The authors of the meta-analysis concluded that "talk appears to play a fundamental role in text-based comprehension" (761).

For teaching moves that scaffold students toward independent talk

see Section 3, page 55

Text discussions can enhance critical thinking, metacognition, and the ability to structure arguments. Small-group student book discussions can be teacher- or student-directed. Student-directed discussions may lead to more sophisticated responses on the part of students (Almasi 1995; Chinn, Anderson, and Waggoner 2001) and situations where students facilitate their own learning (McMahon and Goatley 1995), but teacher scaffolding and facilitation is an important component of development of such discussions (Maloch 2005; McIntyre, Kyle, and Moore 2006).

Approaches like Reciprocal Teaching (Palincsar and Brown 1984) and literature circles (Daniels 2002) scaffold students toward independent talk. Reciprocal Teaching is the discussion of a text based on four reading strategies—questioning, clarifying, summarizing, and predicting. These strategies help students monitor and develop their own comprehension. At first, the teacher models the strategies and the teacher and students share in conversation, but this leads to student-led discussion. Literature circles are small, student-led group discussions that are initially scaffolded by roles such as summarizer; the scaffold is removed as students gain confidence and skill at text discussion. Small-group text discussions focused on problem solving are especially beneficial (Soter and Rudge 2005). These brief literature discussions can reengage students during IR, which is a perennial concern with teachers (Bryan, Fawson, and Reutzel 2003). Nystrand (2006) found that even as little as ten minutes of peer discussion around texts improved standardized test scores for students. For more information on these strategies, see *Questioning the Author* (Beck et al. 1997), *Reciprocal Teaching at Work* (Oczkus 2010), and *Literature Circles* (Daniels 2002).

Why Independent Reading Matters Most for Striving Readers and English Learners

Because striving readers spend less time in classrooms actually reading, they are in dire need of the reading practice that IR provides. Poor readers read far fewer words in school than good ones, seldom read silently, and get less comprehension strategy instruction than better readers.

(See Allington 2013 for further discussion of this.) Although setting aside time for more reading does not *always* help low achievers learn to read (Marshall 2002), numerous studies have concluded that below-level readers, English learners, learning disabled students, and average readers benefit more from being given opportunities to read than other readers (Lewis 2002; Manning, Lewis, and Lewis 2010).

Striving readers can increase their reading achievement through IR under certain specific conditions. Kamil (2008), for example, studied the impact of elementary students' (grades 2–6) recreational reading of informational texts on reading fluency, comprehension, and vocabulary. Participants included large numbers of English learners (61 percent in some schools) and a large percentage of striving readers. There was no specific time set aside for IR, but students were encouraged to read during school time other than instructional (lunch, before and after school, during breaks, and out of school). The study included a reading incentive program called California Reads that provides students with motivation and rewards for reading. Two school districts participated in the study, and participants at each school were assigned to one of three groups:

- Group 1 received the incentive program, informational books, and ongoing teacher professional development designed to help teachers support students in reading informational texts.
- Group 2 received the books and incentive program, but no professional development.
- Group 3, the control group, received no books, no incentives, and no professional development.

Students in the first group showed significant gains in both fluency and comprehension. The incentive program and books alone were not enough to increase achievement. Echoing the findings of previously mentioned studies, the author concluded that recreational reading *coupled with instruction* and professional development can improve reading achievement for all students, including English learners, but that mere print exposure is insufficient.

One of the most interesting findings of the research is that many of the IR activities suggested in this section, such as small-group instruction, are even more beneficial for striving readers than for average and above-average readers. However, for striving readers to succeed during IR, they need more supports than they are often getting from teachers during IR. They need more:

- help in selecting books (Reutzel, Fawson, and Smith 2008)
- time for reading in and out of school (Allington 2009)
- during reading support (Reis et al. 2007)
- instruction focused on reading strategies (Allington 2012)
- opportunities for small group discussions (Soter et al. 2008)

Engaging striving readers in IR with differentiated support can help ensure that these children receive literacy learning experiences that are more, rather than less, comparable to their peers in terms of time spent reading, quality instruction, and differentiated support.

The Last Word: An Overview of Independent Reading Implementation by Teachers

In most of the studies in this section, researchers initiated specific IR interventions to test specific hypotheses. Not surprisingly, a study of highly effective elementary teachers revealed consistent patterns of effective IR practice (Sanden 2012). Sherry Sanden spent six months observing, interviewing, and collecting materials from eight elementary literacy teachers and their students about their daily uses of IR. The focus teachers who were identified by their principals as highly effective literacy teachers worked in grades 1 through 5 and taught in urban, rural, and suburban schools across the country. She found that these teachers "were united in their beliefs about the necessity of adult support . . . and ongoing assistance in areas such as monitoring student choices, teaching IR behaviors, and maintaining a focus on student growth" (7). We can examine these teachers' practices to give us an overview of effective IR.

First, these teachers encouraged self-selection of books based on interest, but carefully matched readers to books of appropriate difficulty. The teachers encouraged the reading of multiple text types and provided many suggestions for book titles. They modeled appropriate IR behaviors, demonstrating to students what an independent reader looks like, providing a poster listing appropriate IR reading behaviors, and showing students how to locate a reading spot. Reading experiences were appropriate to student ages; younger children read orally or whisper read and teachers sometimes paired students for IR. They also provided direct, embedded instruction in reading strategies during large-group lessons, individual conferences, and other IR events.

These teachers required student accountability through products such as reading logs, written responses, and story summaries. They also used large- and small-group book discussions and individual student conferences; their monitoring of student progress was ongoing. Interestingly, not one of these teachers read independently during IR; instead, they provided the kinds of multiple supports identified by the research as requisites for effective IR.

To sum it up, for IR to succeed, the teacher must be an active participant. She cannot sit on the sidelines and just watch what is going on, or sit reading or grading papers: she must bring all her teaching talents to bear during IR just as during any other instructional activity. As Reutzel, Jones, and Newman (2010) put it: "[Effective] independent silent reading practice actively involves teachers in structuring, guiding, teaching, interacting with, monitoring and holding students accountable for time spent reading independently and silently" (176).

In Section 3, you will learn about practices like the ones the effective teachers in this study used to make IR successful. These will help you create a classroom where IR flourishes and kids build the skills they need to discover the love of reading.

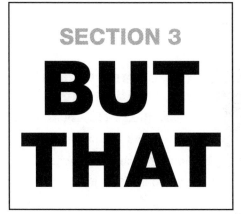

SECTION 3

BUT THAT

An Instructional Framework for Supporting Classroom Independent Reading

DEBBIE MILLER

Now let's get back to Baltimore and crab cakes. As the evening grew longer, teachers became more and more committed to making the time for independent reading (IR). They'd known all along that something wasn't right about how they were teaching reading, and now they knew just what it was. Once they were determined to figure out how to put IR into an instructional framework, I knew then and there that it was going to happen.

In Section 2, you read a compelling argument for *why* IR should happen in the classroom and the practices that show you *how* to make IR effective for all your students; now you'll learn how to coordinate those practices in your classroom. The direct link between strong instruction and follow-up in independent work is a key component of IR.

We'll catch up with the Baltimore teachers in a bit, but first, let's take a quick look at a typical day in the reading block. Then we'll return to the important questions about finding time for more IR and explore a wide range of engaging, research-based principles and tactics you can use to help you and your children make the most of IR time.

For the research that explains the value of classroom time reading

see Section 2, page 16

A Recommended Day in the Reading Block

• **First, there's a focus lesson.** Children gather together in large or small groups, and teachers explicitly teach them what readers do and how they do it. These lessons are well planned, short, and focused, and teachers explicitly teach children what they want their students to learn how to do, explain why it's important, and show them how it will help them as readers.

• **Following the lesson, children spend time reading and practicing what their teacher has just shown them how to do.** Students work to apply what we've just taught them, and they read and practice in a range of real books and materials that are worthy of what their teacher is asking them to do. Teachers confer with children during this time, monitor their progress, and give them opportunities to write and talk about their books and big ideas.

IR doesn't always mean reading in isolation. As we saw in Section 2, children need to have purposeful conversations with each other about their books, whether it's talking with a partner or participating in a book club. Both of these important practices occur during this time.

• **Right after IR, children come back together to share their reflections about their reading and what they learned about themselves as readers that day, particularly as it connects to the focus lesson.** For example, if the lesson is about how readers pay attention to what the main characters say and do to help them determine the big ideas in their stories, this is what we confer with children about, and this will also be the focus of the share.

We've come full circle now—children have had explicit teaching in a focus lesson, they have had opportunities during IR to practice applying it, and now they come back together to talk about what they've discovered. These daily opportunities for teaching and learning set this instructional framework apart from programs like Drop Everything and Read (DEAR) and Sustained Silent Reading.

Known by many as readers' workshop, this framework is based on the principles of time, choice, response, and community, and it allows for in-depth teaching and learning, flexibility, differentiation, and ultimately, independence. (See Figure 3–1.)

Figure 3–1

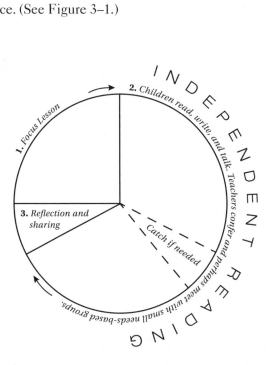

Strive for a one third–two thirds balance in your readers' workshop—one third of the time is designated for explicit teaching, and the remaining two thirds of the time is devoted to IR, writing, talking, conferring, and perhaps a small, needs-based group. Remember—children learn to read in significant part by reading—the more they read, the better they get.

Now let's return to the problem of time and your classroom. Are you, just like our colleagues in Baltimore, up for a fact-finding mission of your own? If so, get with a colleague, or better yet, colleagues, and ask yourselves, "What are our kids doing from the early morning hellos to the end-of-day good-byes?" Be objective—what things are absolutely essential to ensure student learning, growth, and success? Do you believe that each child is positioned to achieve at least a year's growth in their time with you?

Might there be activities or actions that could be tweaked or eliminated to ensure that no child falls through the cracks? You might do a four-column note activity (below) in your notebook to help you—maybe you'll be surprised, just like my friends in Baltimore were when they did this activity, at just where those minutes were hiding!

Try It: Evaluate Your Time			
Make a list: What exactly are children doing during your reading block of time? What about the rest of the day?	What things on your list help children grow as readers and learners? What doesn't?	Depending on your answers, decide: What stays? What goes? Cross out what needs to go and add up your found minutes.	The Big Reveal—How many minutes did you find? Nice work! Now, let's think about how to use them wisely.

Let's look at where we found the time to implement this instructional framework for IR.

How Much Time Did We Find?

Remember all the activities that stood in the way of IR in Section 1? After some serious soul-searching and analyzing their literacy schedule based on our fact-finding mission and the preceding table, the teachers in Baltimore made significant modifications to how they used to do things, and removed some practices altogether—particularly from the reading block. Across the grades, teachers were able to find an additional 60 to 125 minutes a day!

What happened? Where did all those minutes come from?

Calendar activities. What happened?

Calendar activities were streamlined to ten minutes at most. And all of the Paddys now reside in the kindergarten classrooms, where they are part of a center activity.

Minutes found? Fifteen to twenty. Maybe that doesn't sound like much in a day, but think about this: It's at least 75 minutes a week, 300 minutes a month, and a whopping 2,700 minutes in a school year!

Morning announcements. What happened?

The principal decided to eliminate the morning announcements altogether and instead email the particulars to teachers each morning. Teachers promised to share pertinent information with their children when they saw fit, and it was posted in the office and on the school website for all to see. Also, intercom interruptions throughout the day ("Finley in room 107—could you please meet your mother in the office?") were also eliminated whenever possible.

Minutes found? Ten to fifteen. Not to mention the minutes teachers and children spent just waiting for the morning announcements to start so they could begin their day!

Transitions. What happened?

Many teachers opted to play music for transitions instead of flicking the lights, counting to ten, and so on. Children learned that when they hear the music playing, that's a signal to stop what they're doing, put their things away, and gather in the meeting area, or wherever the teacher designates. The only rule here is that everyone has gathered, or is ready for next steps, by the time the song is over. Early birds get to sing along. Simple!

Minutes found? About two. But the music was calming for children *and* teachers, providing a stress-free, joyful transition.

Lining up. What happened?

Lining up in the described ways (if you're wearing red, etc.) was abandoned. We asked children in all grades to observe how people line up outside of school, and do it that way in school, too. (No line leaders, give way if someone is getting in line at the same time you are, be courteous, walk, no boys' line and girls' line.) Authenticity rules!

Minutes found? Twelve to fifteen throughout the day.

Packing up to go home. What happened?

Teachers reduced the amount of time for getting ready to go home. And lunch. And specials.

Minutes found? Five to ten.

The Reading Block. What happened?

This block of time was completely restructured. By the end of the year, readers' workshop was up and running in every classroom, K–5. Centers, worksheets, and other "keeping kids busy" activities were mostly eliminated in favor of explicit teaching, IR and conferring, and time for children to reflect and share their learning. Centers were kept in kindergarten and one first-grade classroom, but they were separate from the workshop.

Minutes found? Thirty to sixty.

DEAR Time. What happened?

DEAR time as described was eliminated in all classrooms.

Minutes found? Twenty.

Note: Some teachers wanted to include recreational reading within the school day, and with distinct modifications to the old DEAR time, it was lovely. These teachers chose to begin the first twenty minutes of the day with IR—children came in, got their books, and started reading. Music played softly, children read in comfy chairs, at their tables, and on the floor, and they talked with each other and their teacher about their reading. This time was in *addition* to IR minutes within the literacy block and the content areas.

Making the Most of Independent Reading

So now that we've found the minutes, how do we use them well? Maybe you worry that IR time will be a long, silent slog and wonder how on earth your children can sustain reading for thirty, forty-five, or sixty minutes. But stay with me! We realize—and we've seen the research that supports this in Section 2—that IR needs to be an active, engaging, and joyful (yes, joyful!) time of day.

We have to be careful (and vigilant) not to go back to centers, worksheets, and all those other "keeping kids busy" kinds of activities we talked about in Section 1. To make sure I don't ever go back, I use four principles (see Figure 3–2) to guide me in making decisions about what's worthy of children's time during IR time:

The research that informs these principles is explained

see Section 2, pages 15–19

Figure 3–2 Guiding Principles for Instruction

Guiding Principles for Instruction
Purpose—What are students working toward? What are our learning goals?
Authenticity—Does the work that I'm asking my students to do happen in the world, *outside* the classroom?
Choice—Do students have opportunities to make choices about what to read, where to read, and with whom?
Explicit Instruction—How will I show, model, or demonstrate just what I want children to practice and learn how to do?

Provide Purpose: What, How, and Why Readers Read

The first thing we need to do when launching students' IR lives is to give children real reasons to read. I want them to be clear about questions like these:

> What's my purpose for my reading today?
>
> What am I going to try to figure out?
>
> How will I demonstrate my understanding of my/our learning goal?

and

> I wonder what I will learn about myself as a reader today?
>
> What will I get smarter about?

When teachers are explicit and children have a clear purpose for their reading work each day, it engages and motivates them to want to read and work hard. This is all about student ownership of learning. We're asking children to practice and discover the work real readers do, how they think, and how reading makes us smarter and more powerful in the world.

And following IR, when children understand that they have the chance every day to come back together and reflect on what they've learned and how they've grown as readers that day, this also connects to purpose—children have a forum where they can discuss what they've learned and how they've gotten smarter as readers this day.

Keep It Authentic: Do Readers Do This in the World?

When I'm planning my lessons, I want to make certain that the kinds of things I'm asking children to do are the kinds of things that they will encounter outside the classroom doors—I want them to learn to do the kinds of things independent readers do in real life. So I'm always asking myself, "Does what I'm thinking about asking children to do happen in the world? Is this something *I* do outside of school?" If I can answer yes, it's most likely a go. If I answer no, I simply am not going there. Let me show you what I mean. How would *you* answer these questions about your reading life?

Do I fill out worksheets after reading a book?

Do I choose the books I read?

Do I keep a list of books I've read and want to read? If not, do I know people who do?

Do I answer someone else's questions after I finish reading?

Do I make made posters about books when I finish reading? What about dioramas?

Do I recommend books to friends and colleagues?

Do I talk with someone about what I've read?

Do I always read books that are at my level? Do I ever read something that's easy? Challenging?

Do I belong to a book group? If not, do I know people who do?

Do I write a summary every time I finish reading a book?

Do I ever annotate, or write questions, responses, and so on in the margins of my books or on sticky notes?

Do I ask questions, make connections, and infer big ideas *at the same time I'm reading?*

So—what did you discover? What things are a "go" for you? What things are a big, fat no?

Support Choice: Teach Students How to Choose Books

As Barb explained in Section 2, choice is an essential to IR. Because of the direct link between strong instruction and guided and independent practice, children need books that are worthy of what we are asking them to do. For example, if

Why is choice important? For the research that supports student choice

see Section 2, pages 16–20

the lesson is about learning what readers do when they come to a word they don't know, every child will need a book(s) where they can read most of the words, but not all of them. If their book is too easy, they may not have an opportunity to practice what we're working to teach them. They won't get smarter about themselves as readers that day.

Or say it's a series of comprehension lessons—if the books and/or materials children are reading don't give them something to think *about,* they won't get smarter about themselves on that day, either. See Figure 3–3.

Figure 3–3 Questions to Ask When Choosing Books

Questions Students Can Ask Themselves When Choosing Books
I teach children to ask themselves four things when it comes to choosing books: • Am I interested in this book? • Can I read it? • Does it give me something to think and talk about? • Will it help me practice what I'm/we're learning how to do?

To make the kinds of choices that keep them engaged during IR and growing as readers, teachers need to give children many opportunities to get to know themselves as readers and explicitly show them how to make wise decisions. Whether it's about where to sit, who to work with, or what to read (Guthrie and Humenick 2004), I intervene when children's choices are off the mark. Teaching children to make wise choices takes time, energy, persistence, and practice. For example, if a child's book is not going to move her forward as a reader, it's not about taking the child's book away—it's talking with the child about her choice and working together to help her find a better match. If all else fails, I choose three books that I know would be just right (and hopefully interesting to the child) and say, "You pick one." For questions to consider when guiding student choice, see Figure 3–4.

Figure 3–4 Questions to Guide Student Choice

Questions to Consider When Guiding Student Choice

Remember—the term *just right* is fluid—it depends on what children are working toward. As you help children choose, consider:

- Could a book that's easy to read be just right for a child working on fluency?

- Could a book above a child's level be just right if he has extensive background about its content and/or is highly motivated to read it?

- Could a book be just right for a child working on comprehension if the words are easy to read, but the content is challenging?

- Could a book be just right for a child working on decoding if she knows most of the words, but not all of them, and the content is easy?

- Could a challenging book be just right for the child who is highly motivated to read it?

- Could a book that's easy to read be just right for the child who needs to build background knowledge on a specific topic?

Provide Explicit Instruction About What, How, and Why Readers Read

Children don't necessarily come to us knowing how readers make meaning, how to talk about texts in meaningful ways, or the conversational moves they can make to take the conversation deeper. What can teachers do? We show children how.

What does research have to say about strategy instruction?

see Section 2, pages 19

Demonstrate how readers make meaning. Let children in on how readers make meaning by thinking aloud about how *you* make meaning. When you do—when you make your mental processes visible— you show children what good thinking sounds like, why it's important, and just how they can begin to apply it on their own or with a partner during IR time. Be precise when you think aloud—use real language and standard terminology—what you say and how you say it quickly becomes what they say and how they say it.

For an explanation of why students need exposure to a variety of genres and genre-specific reading instruction

see Section 2, pages 19–20, 22–23

Provide reasons to read a variety of text topics and genres and genre-specific reading instruction. Through read-alouds and your classroom library, give children exposure to lots of different kinds of text, let them know the different reasons for reading specific texts, and provide instruction so that students know what to expect when they encounter comics, magazines, pop-culture titles, fantasy, biographies, poetry, graphic novels, realistic fiction, informational texts, and online texts.

When writing in these different genres, authors use different tools and structures to communicate ideas. Students need more than one text exposure to each genre so that they can learn the variety of ways these tools and structures can be used, as well as practice the different genre-specific strategies for reading the variety of informational texts (for example) that they'll encounter in the world. By tracking which genres are being read, students can self-monitor their genre preferences and genres they haven't yet tried, and the teacher can attend to the genre choices for read-aloud and the kinds of text tools and structures students need to learn about.

For the research that supports talk as a scaffold for independent reading

see Section 2, pages 35–36

Model how to talk about texts. Reading is a social activity. We do this as adults all the time, and it's just the kind of accountable talk the Common Core State Standards requires of our students. (See the Speaking and Listening Standards for details.) As Barb explained in Section 2, talking about texts together not only improves comprehension and makes children aware of how they can use strategies according to the kind of text and the demands it places on them as readers, but also motivates them to read independently so that they'll have something to talk about with their peers. Students need teacher scaffolds toward independent talk. With time and practice, student discussion of texts embodies the ideal of authentic conversation: responsive, thoughtful, and expansive.

Read-alouds offer us the perfect opportunity to structure meaningful talk around a text. Use powerful picture books and set the thinking bar high. Model your thinking, and invite children into the discussion early and often, and listen carefully to what they say. Model some more. Invite them back into the conversation. Here, children are responsible for the thinking, not the reading. They learn conversational moves that will support independent talk with their peers and thinking moves that will help them during their IR work (see Figure 3–5). You'll be surprised by their insights, particularly when your book choices focus on interesting, compelling topics and big ideas.

> **To learn about the researched models that inform this instruction— Instructional Conversations, Questioning the Author, literature circles, and Reciprocal Teaching**
>
> see Section 2, pages 35–36

Intentional and instructional moves like these pave the way for purposeful turning and talking, small-group work, partner reading and thinking, book clubs, and ultimately independence. After all, our goal is for students to get together *on their own* to talk about books and big ideas. For more information on a variety of researched approaches to support independent talk, see the following resources:

Questioning the Author (Beck et al. 1997)
Reciprocal Teaching at Work (Oczkus 2010)
Literature Circles (Daniels 2002)

Figure 3–5 Modeling Conversational and
Thinking Moves During Read-Aloud

Modeling Conversational and Thinking Moves During Read-Aloud
When a child shares her thinking during a whole-class discussion, I might say:

> Does anyone have anything to say to Eliot that will extend her thinking, and ours? Frankie—you do? Let's try it. Look at Eliot. (Everyone, let's listen in to this conversation and see what we can learn.) Now connect your thinking to hers—say, "When you said . . . it made me think about. . . ."

After Frankie shares her thinking with Eliot, I say, "So what do you think? What will you say back to Frankie?"

Or, I might ask questions like:

> Who has a different point of view?
>
> What in the text is making you think that?
>
> Say more about that.

Turn and talk. I often ask children to turn and talk with a partner about something specific during the read-aloud. For example, if we're working on identifying character traits, I might say, "Everyone—take a minute to think about what we know about Nasreen's grandmother [in the book, *Nasreen's Secret School* by Jeannette Winter (2009)]. Based on what we've learned about her so far in the story, what kind of a person is she? What words would you use to describe her? Is she like another character you know? Turn and talk with your partner about your thinking."

Again, children are responsible for the thinking, not the reading, and turning and talking is a great way to release responsibility to children and give them opportunities to learn and practice accountable talk and the civility of conversation. Turn and talk prepares students for student-led small-group discussions, which I'll explain later in this section. It

Figure 3–6 As students turn and talk, here's what the teacher can do

What a Teacher Can Do While Students Turn and Talk
What's the teacher doing while students are turning and talking? She's up and out of her chair and listening in, thinking to herself: • Are student conversations focused? • Are they referring back to the text? • Are they listening closely to each other and practicing conversational moves? • Are there misconceptions? • Do children need more or less modeling?

might be messy and it'll probably take more time than you'd like, but stay the course. Come January, you'll be happy you did!

Now that we've discussed four guiding principles for IR, let's talk about specific tactics we can put into play to keep children motivated, engaged, and focused during IR.

Tactics Teachers Can Use to Keep Things Hopping During IR

Tactic 1: Get books in their hands. The IR goals are the same for every child, but children *apply* their learning in books and materials that are just right for them. That's why classroom libraries are essential—you'll need a wide range of texts and levels to ensure that all children have books that meet their needs and allow them to participate fully as readers and learners. I'm aware of what the research says about the number of books we should have, but in my experience, those numbers are low. I'd strive for at least one thousand books, and I wouldn't stop there. But don't be disheartened— classroom libraries aren't built in a day. Here are a few surefire ways to get started.

For an explanation of the importance of providing access to books

see Section 2, page 27

Shop in your school first. Check out closets, cupboards, and that little room next to the gym that's been locked for years because nobody knows where the key is. (In Baltimore, we found tubs and tubs of songbooks, predictable books, and books written for beginning readers in that little room. Now *Brown Bear, Brown Bear, What Do You See?* [Martin 1967] is back in children's hands, along with *The Lady with the Alligator Purse* [Westcott 1998], *This Land Is Your Land* [Guthrie 2010], and those famous friends, Frog and Toad [Lobel].)

Once you and your colleagues have searched high and low for books, spread them out and see what you have. What stays—what's worthy of children's time and attention? What goes—what isn't?

Also, do you have a book room? They're often filled with shelves and shelves of leveled texts, but sometimes it looks as if these books haven't been used at all! What's keeping teachers from getting them off the shelves and into the hands of kids? Is the sign-out complicated? Are we afraid we might lose one? Is it just too much hassle? I say take what you need, sign them out so others know where they are, and keep them as long as you need them.

Fully utilize school and local libraries, and appreciate librarians! They know books, and they love children and teachers. Once they understand why you want to check out one hundred books for a four-week social studies unit on immigration, they'll be more than willing to gather them for you. (And more often than not, late fees—not that you'd have any—will be waived.) Put a volunteer on it, and voilà! You've got books!

Take advantage of book club points (Scholastic, etc.). Google "free books for kids" and see what comes up. Appeal to your PTA and local businesses. Write grants. Great books are out there. They might as well be yours.

Consider your needs. Now that your books are organized and you know what you have, think about what you need. Think: What books and materials do you and children need to teach and learn well? Think about the fifty-fifty balance between literary and informational text (Common Core State Standard Document). Consider your social studies and science content—begin to collect books that children can dig into and read during those allocated times. Make a list of books you need and keep it ready. You never know when you'll get that urgent email from the office saying that $250 must be spent by 3:15 *today!*

Tactic 2: Organize your books for easy access. Buy plastic tubs at the dollar store, spread out the books you have, and figure out (yourself, or even better, with your kids) how to best organize them. You'll want to have some leveled texts, as well as a range and variety of books organized by author, genre, big ideas, topic, and so on. You also might consider organizing some of these books in different ways, particularly the nonfiction texts on popular topics. What if the reptile books were put together in one tub, regardless of level? That way anyone in the classroom who's interested in reptiles (or any topic) could have easy access and get together in small groups based on interest, rather than level. And what about the class sets of books like *Charlotte's Web* (White 2006), *The Secret Garden* (Burnett 2005), and *Because of Winn-Dixie* (DiCamillo 2010) that line shelf after shelf? How about placing several copies of each set in the appropriate classrooms?

Tactic 3: Start with small chunks of classroom IR time. After explicit instruction, let children have at it, and confer with them to see how they're doing. Our job as teachers is to listen to children, learn from them, and teach them something they need to know to move forward and accomplish their goals.

As Barb explained in Section 2, the amount of time a student should spend on IR depends on the child. We can't force a reluctant student reader to read for forty-five minutes straight—that's no way to teach a child to love reading! But we can ensure that reluctant readers have an array of interesting texts in their stack of books, just like everyone else. Some of their texts will be leveled, but they, too, need a range of texts that they have chosen and are excited about learning to read.

If IR is something new for children (and you!), you might start out with just ten or fifteen minutes, and increase the minutes over time. Give yourself and your students a couple of weeks or so, and you'll be there before you know it. You'll find that if students have access to books they are interested in, books they can read with accuracy, fluency, and comprehension, *and* books that give them something to think about, getting them to read for longer and longer periods of time won't be a problem. Instead, you'll have a more pleasant problem—they won't want to stop! (This is also true for our most reluctant readers—the book is often the hook.)

The best way to build stamina is through engagement. When we ensure that students have access to an array of interesting texts, it produces reading achievement gains roughly four times as large as the small effect of systematic phonics instruction as reported by the National Reading Panel (Guthrie and Humenick 2004).

Tactic 4: Monitor IR. How do we monitor student progress during IR, and how do these actions help us differentiate wisely? First, we're present. We don't want passivity from children, and we definitely don't want passivity from ourselves. Present teachers are active teachers—they're tuned in to children and responsive to their needs as learners.

Taking a minute or two during IR to step back and observe children as a whole gives us instant, important information. Who's engaged? Who isn't? How do we know? Who are we not sure of? Monitoring student actions and behaviors, and then conferring with those who need our encouragement and support, is what intentional teaching is all about. Simply asking, "I'm noticing you're having a hard time today—What's going on? How can I help?" lets children know we've noticed something is amiss, we care about them as readers and learners and people, and we want to help.

Maybe we discover it's about book selection. Maybe what we've asked children to do is too easy or too hard. Or just maybe a child isn't feeling well. We'll never know unless we take the time to notice, find out why, and take positive action. Putting a check mark on the board next to the child's name or reprimanding a child isn't what monitoring is all about. It's less about what the child is doing, and more about why. And doing what we can to help.

Figure 3–7   Guidelines for Monitoring Student IR

Guidelines for Monitoring Student IR
• We also are monitoring when we pay attention to:
• The books children are reading—have they included a balance of genres, authors, and levels of difficulty? Do their books give them something to think about? Are children consistently moving forward and showing growth as readers?
• Children's reading logs—are their responses growing increasingly more sophisticated? Are they focused less on retelling and more on big ideas? (See Tactic 7: Invite students to reflect on and share their learning, for more information.)
• Their conversations with each other—are they participating and engaged? Are they open to perspectives that are different from their own? Do they refer back to the text to cite evidence that supports their thinking?

Tactic 5: Differentiate instruction and create accountability through conferring. Monitoring helps you decide which students you'll confer with. When you confer, you are actively gathering information about how they're reading and what they need to grow as readers. Conferring is as much about information gathering as it is about instruction, and when you first start IR with your students, conferences are mostly about listening. How do students view reading? How do they view themselves as readers? What are they interested in?

Early conferences are all about building relationships with children, establishing trust, and getting to know and love them. Later, conferences will focus on listening to children talk about their reading and thinking (particularly how it connects to the focus lesson/learning goal), learning what they need to move forward, teaching, and goal setting.

Figure 3–8 Sample Conferring Questions

Sample Questions for Conferring
What kinds of books do you like best? Why?
What are you reading now? What books do you have in your stack? (If I get a blank look, I say, "So if you *had* a stack, what books might be there, just waiting for you to read?")
What do you know about what readers do? (Blank look? Ask, "Is there someone you know who reads a lot? What does that person do?")
What's one thing I should know about you as a reader?
How can I help you grow as a reader?

Conferring is differentiation at its finest! When we confer with children one-to-one, we're working hard to personalize our instruction and support children as they apply what we've taught them in large- and small-group settings. Teachers and children can set and record individual goals for students during this time to help ensure that no child falls through the cracks, and all children grow as independent readers.

I take notes when I confer with children, writing what I notice and learn about them as readers. I use this information to set goals with children, share with parents during conferences, and inform small-group instruction. For example, if I notice there are children who have similar needs, I'll bring them together, out of efficiency, for more explicit instruction. These children won't be at the same level, they'll be brought together because of need.

As we learned from Barb in Section 2, striving readers and English language learners spend less time than other children in classrooms actually reading, even when we know that IR benefits them greatly. Reading workshop is perfectly positioned to meet their needs: time to read, support from their teacher during reading, explicit instruction on reading strategies, and opportunities for small-group discussions. Reading workshop is not the time to pull out English language learners or striving readers. Or anyone else.

Tactic 6: Use a catch to refocus the group. What if I notice that student stamina is fading? Or learn something from conferring or listening in that would be important for everyone to know? Instead of addressing these issues during reflection and share time, or in a lesson the next day, now I attend to them right then and there, when my actions and words can be most useful and powerful. Bringing children back together, *briefly* addressing what they need to do or think about to move forward, then sending them back to work, breathes energy, life, and a renewed sense of purpose into IR time (Miller 2013, 12).

For example, let's say you've just taught a lesson about asking questions in informational texts, and children are now reading independently and writing their questions on sticky notes. As you confer, you're noticing that more than a few children are recording questions that they already know the answer to—not a good thing! So, let's "catch" everyone back together and talk about it. Model your questions—maybe from one of the books a child is reading—and send them off again.

Tactic 7: Invite students to reflect on and share their learning.
What will children do when they finish a book? How will they track their reading? Where will they read? Be clear about questions like these and let them know precisely what you expect of them during this time and what they can expect from you. This is really all about student ownership of learning.

When children track their reading over time, they have a clear picture of the types of texts they've read, how hard they've worked, their thinking about their reading, and so on. For example, in Barb Smith's classroom, she helps students not only track their reading but reflect and set goals for themselves based on what they're noticing from their book logs. (See Figure 3–9 for examples of student reflection and Figure 3–10 for questions to guide students during student reflection time.)

Figure 3–9a   Student Reflection

Name _Kiana_   **My Reading Log**

Date	Title	Genre
12-14-12	Animal hospital	Nf
12-17-12	Santa mouse and the ratdeer	f
12-17-12	Survivors the night the Titanic sank	Nf
12-17-12	The story of Anne Frank	Nf
12-18-12	II	Nf
12-19-12	Bermuda triangle	Nf
12-20-12	II	Nf
1-9-13	Dinosaur detectives	Nf
1-10-13	II	Nf
1-11-13	Vanished the mysterious disappearance of	Nf

Figure 3–9b

Name _Kiaorece_   1/8/13 ✓

Stop and Reflect on Your Reading

Look through your reading log and write down two things you noticed.

I noticed _I'm reading a lot of fiction._

I noticed _I'm reading a lot of easy books._

Goal: What is one thing you **want to do or work on** in the next month?

Read different genres that are just right books   **poetry**

Figure 3–9c

Name _Kiana_   **My Reading Log**

Date	Title	Genre
1-11-13	Guess who's coming to Santa's for dinner	F
1-15-13	Secrets of the mummies	Nf
1-30-13	''	Nf
1-30-13	No more homework no more tests	P
2-4-13	''	P
2-6-13	Where the sidewalk ends	P
2-7-13	''	P
2-8-13	''	P
2-11-13	''	P
2-12-13	''	P

Figure 3–10   Questions to Guide Student Reflection on IR

Questions to Guide Student Reflection on IR
• What did you do to get smarter today?
• What do you understand now that you didn't understand before? How did you figure it out?
• What did you learn about yourself as a reader that you will do in the days and weeks to come?

Tactic 8: Use partner reading and book clubs to get students talking and reading independently. After experiencing book talk through read-aloud and turn and talk during explicit instruction, children are ready for independent talk. I teach them to read a page or two, then stop and think together, read some more, and stop and think together some more. And then I ask, "So what do you understand now (after talking with your partner) that you didn't understand before? Who can be specific about this?" If children have trouble, try to give them a scaffolded frame like "I used to think . . . then I talked with _____ and she said . . . and now I'm thinking. . . ."

Partner reading is the perfect time to integrate the comprehension and collaboration standards, as well as many reading standards, preparing children for independent work and book clubs.

Now, because children have had daily opportunities for extensive IR, they are ready to fully participate in thoughtful, constructive conversations about the same text in book clubs. To prepare them for this new level of independence, I review expectations for book clubs (see Figure 3–11). You can also help scaffold this experience by offering up specific choices for book clubs (see Figure 3–12).

Tactic 9: Assess students' progress as independent readers.

When teachers and children truly share in the responsibility for children's learning, it's about shared ownership for growth over time. I want children to be aware of what they can do today that they couldn't do yesterday, and to be aware of the processes they used—exactly what they did—to get there. I want them to have evidence that all their effort and hard work has paid off and that there is purpose in what I've asked them to do.

Figure 3–11 **Expectations for Book Club Conversations**

Expectations for Book Club Conversations
• We come prepared—we've read the book, or up to a certain amount of pages.
• We keep track of our thinking, and the important parts/points we want to discuss.
• We practice our conversational moves and the civility of conversation.
• We're open to new perspectives and add to the ideas of others.
• We agree and disagree, and explain what in the text makes us think this way.
• We come ready to participate, listen, and learn.

Figure 3–12 Tips for Book Club Text Choices

Some Tips for Book Club Text Choices

When offering up book choices for book clubs, consider a range of thought-provoking picture books (fiction and nonfiction), short stories, novels, and even poetry selections for children to choose from.

And don't forget wordless books! In a short residency at SOAR Elementary School in Denver, my friend Samantha Bennett and I introduced book clubs to Hannah Whittaker's third graders using wordless books. The books we chose for this short immersion were on the big ideas around "taking a stand" through the issues of:

War	*Trafalgar and Waterloo* by Oliver Tallec
	Why? by Nicolai Popov
The Underground Railroad	*Unspoken* by Henry Cole
Unconventional friendships	*The Lion and The Mouse* by Jerry Pinkney
	A Circle of Friends by Giora Carmi
Immigration	*The Arrival* by Shaun Tan
Bullying	*No!* by David McPhail

In the examples in Figure 3–13, you see how these matching assessments for learning give teachers and children reliable information about where the child is now (in relationship to the learning goal) and what the child and what the teacher needs to do to close the gap. This is the best way I know to ensure that every child grows as an independent reader every day.

Figure 3–13 Creating Informal Formative Assessments

Learning Goal	Matching Assessment for Learning
I can ask important questions about a topic I care about.	Sticky notes
I can explain what I need to do to work hard and get smarter in readers' workshop.	"Thinking about myself as a reader" reflection sheet
I can think deeply about a topic and ask important questions.	Notebook entries

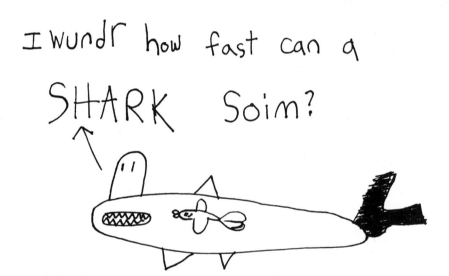

Cora's sticky note (kindergarten)

My name __Grace__

Thinking about Myself as a Reader

I look like this when I am an active, engaged reader.

Three things that help me work smart as a reader are:

1. Wt he room is
⊗uit.
2. Wh the Bok is
ese.
3. I foc is.

Grace's reflection sheet (grade 1)

I can think deeply about a topic, and ask important
questions.

Mexico
• Is it one of the best places to go to ?
• Does it have awesome teachers that you
just have to go see ?

• Why was it known as Tenochtitlan ?

• Why Is immagration a really
big deal in Mexico ?

• Why was there olny a little bit of
people who were wealthy ?

• Why aren't there alot of jobs in
Mexico ?

Andrew's notebook entry (grade 4)

After looking at the figures, what do you notice about these assessments? Are they open-ended? Do they offer opportunities for every child to be successful? What do they tell us about individual children? What might be their next steps?

Tactic 10: Support independence through assessment choices.
If we're truly working toward IR, we need to give children opportunities to decide how they'll go about sharing their understanding: Is a sticky note just the thing? Does a notebook entry make sense? Will they show what they learned in words, pictures, or pictures and words? Can that demonstration of learning be shown through reflections on their growth

as a reader, in addition to authentic ways that readers communicate their response to texts, such as book reviews for real audiences (blogs, Amazon, or Good Read posts)?

The Kind of Independent Readers We Want Our Students to Be

When I think about the big ideas around reading, and why it matters, I consider not only what I want for my students at the end of the year, but also what I want for them ten years from now, and beyond. I want students to understand:

> Readers read to get smarter and learn about themselves, other people, and the world. Reading is something they can do independently that empowers them to control their lives and make the world a better place.
>
> Readers read, write, think, and learn with purpose and enthusiasm, and see themselves as problem-solving citizens who have what it takes to figure things out.
>
> Readers, writers, and learners engage in conversations and discussions with open hearts and minds, are willing to share their thinking, and appreciate, learn from, and respect the ideas and opinions of others. (Miller 2013, 31)

These big ideas are why IR matters. And this is why, dear reader, I decided to say yes to writing this little book. I want you to embrace the power of IR so that your children will too. Give it a go and see what happens. Take your time. Trust yourself, and trust them. They won't let you down, I promise.

Best wishes, good luck, and happy reading!

AFTERWORD

ELLIN OLIVER KEENE

There is no greater impact on students' reading growth than giving them time to read.

When I first heard these words in 1979, I was truly terrified of the responsibility that had been laid on my shoulders. I was in my first pre-service literacy class and was hoping to learn some kind of magic that I might use in teaching children to read. My professor's words seemed simple, but I knew, even then, that children need the support of clear, focused instruction. However, I wasn't quite sure what that could look like. How I wish I had Debbie and Barbara's book in my hands in 1979!

You've just read Debbie and Barbara's powerful argument for creating literacy blocks: daily time for instruction, content-area learning, goal setting, and practice reading, writing, and talking about books. Children need to see skillful readers at work *and* they need to read with clear goals about how to get better. Choosing what to read and having a sense of agency and social context to their reading lives means that children are engaged when they practice and get better.

What gets in the way of giving students this time? As Debbie demonstrated, evaluating our time can be a gift. Too often, teachers feel that they must keep adding on to their daily schedules, which makes their work increasingly impossible (and less effective). Instead, let's all give ourselves the opportunity to evaluate our time and consider what should go and what should stay. By clearing away the weeds of unproductive activities—do we really need to dress Paddy the Bear?—we create space for students' independent reading to grow and flourish.

This book has invited you to consider which practices and habits may inhibit students' growth as independent readers. School needs to be a place where students fall in love with reading and get better at it. We hope that we've given you the tools to advocate for daily structured time for independent reading. Many of us have long sensed that kids need more time to read but have hesitated to argue for it because we didn't know the research that shows how to make independent reading a joyful, manageable, essential part of their day. Now you know.

REFERENCES

Professional Works Cited

Adams, Marilyn Jager. 2009. "The Challenge of Advanced Texts: The Interdependence of Reading and Learning." In *Reading More, Reading Better*, edited by Elfreida H. Hiebert, 163–89. New York: Guilford.

Ainley, Mary, Suzanne Hidi, and Dagmar Berndorff. 2002. "Interest, Learning, and the Psychological Processes That Mediate Their Relationship." *Journal of Educational Psychology* 94 (3): 545–61.

Allington, Richard. 2002. "What I've Learned About Effective Classroom Teaching from a Decade of Studying Exemplary Elementary School Teachers." *Phi Delta Kappan* 83 (10): 740–47.

———. 2009. "If They Don't Read Much . . . 30 Years Later." In *Reading More, Reading Better*, edited by E. H. Hiebert, 30–54. New York: Guilford.

———. 2011. "Reading Intervention in the Middle Grades." *Voices from the Middle* 19 (2): 10–16.

———. 2012. *What Really Matters for Struggling Readers: Designing Research-Based Programs*. 3d ed. New York: Pearson.

———. 2013. "What Really Matters When Working with Struggling Readers." *The Reading Teacher* 66 (7): 520–30.

Allington, Richard L., Anne McGill-Franzen, Gregory Camilli, Lunetta Williams, Jennifer Graff, Jacqueline Zeig, Courtney Zmach, and Rhonda Nowak. 2010. "Addressing Summer Reading Setback Among Economically Disadvantaged Elementary Students." *Reading Psychology* 31: 411–17.

Allington, Richard L., and Rachael E. Gabriel. 2012. "Every Child, Every Day." *Educational Leadership* 69 (8): 10–15.

Almasi, Janice F. 1995. "The Nature of Fourth Graders' Sociocognitive Conflicts in Peer-Led and Teacher-Led Discussions of Literature." *Reading Research Quarterly* 30: 314–51.

Anderson, Richard C., Paul T. Wilson, and Linda G. Fielding. 1988. "Growth in Reading and How Children Spend Their Time Outside of School." *Reading Research Quarterly* 23 (3): 285–303.

Anderson, Rosemary. 2009. "Interested Reader or Uninterested Dissembler? The Identities Constructed by Upper Primary Aged Dyslexic Pupils During Silent Reading Sessions." *Literacy* 43 (2): 83–90.

Baker, Linda, and Allan Wigfield. 1999. "Dimensions of Children's Motivation for Reading and Their Relations to Reading Activity and Reading Achievement." *Reading Research Quarterly* 34 (4): 452–77.

Beck, Isabel L., Margaret G. McKeown, Rebecca L. Hamilton, and Linda Kucan. 1997. *Questioning the Author: An Approach for Enhancing Student Engagement with Text.* Newark, DE: International Reading Association.

Betts, Emmett A. 1946. *Foundations of Reading Instruction, with Emphasis on Differentiated Guidance.* New York: American Book Company.

Block, Cathy Collins, Cinnamon S. Whiteley, Sherri R. Parris, Kelly L. Reed, and Maggie D. Cleveland. 2009. "Instructional Approaches That Significantly Increase Reading Comprehension." *Journal of Educational Psychology* 101 (2): 262–81.

Block, Cathy Collins, and Michael Pressley. 2007. "Best Practices in Teaching Comprehension." In *Best Practices in Literacy Instruction*, edited by Linda B. Gambrell, Lesley M. Morrow, and Michael Pressley, 220–42. New York: Guilford.

Brenner, Devin, and Elfrieda H. Hiebert. 2010. "If I Follow the Teachers' Editions, Isn't That Enough? Analyzing Reading Volume in Six Core Reading Programs." *The Elementary School Journal* 110 (3): 347–63.

Brenner, Devin, Elfreida H. Hiebert, and Renarta Tompkins. 2009. "How Much and What Are Third Graders Reading? Reading in Core Programs." In *Reading More, Reading Better*, edited by E. H. Hiebert, 118–40. New York: Guilford.

Bryan, Gregory, Parker C. Fawson, and D. Ray Reutzel. 2003. "Sustained Silent Reading: Exploring the Value of Literature Discussion with Three Non-Engaged Readers." *Reading Research and Instruction* 43 (1): 47–73.

Buly, Marsha R., and Shelia W. Valencia. 2002. "Below the Bar: Profiles of Students Who Fail State Reading Tests." *Educational Evaluation and Policy Analysis* 24 (3): 219–39.

Cahill, Carrie, Kathy Horvath, Anne McGill-Franzen, and Richard Allington. 2013. *No More Summer-Reading Loss*. Portsmouth, NH: Heinemann.

Carver, Ronald P., and R. E. Leibert. 1995. "The Effect of Reading Library Books at Different Levels of Difficulty Upon Gain in Reading Ability." *Reading Research Quarterly* 30: 26–48.

Caswell, Linda J., and Nell K. Duke. 1998. "Non-Narrative as a Catalyst for Literacy Development." *Language Arts* 75: 108–77.

Cervetti, Gina N., Marco A. Bravo, Elfreida H. Hiebert, P. David Pearson, and Carolyn A. Jaynes. 2009. "Text Genre and Science Content: Ease of Reading, Comprehension, and Reader Preference." *Reading Psychology* 30 (6): 487–511.

Chinn, Clark A., Richard C. Anderson, and Martha A. Waggoner. 2001. "Patterns of Discourse in Two Kinds of Literature Discussion." *Reading Research Quarterly* 36 (4): 378–411.

Chorzempa, Barbara Fink, and Stephen Graham. 2006. "Primary-Grade Teachers' Use of Within Class Ability Grouping in Reading." *Journal of Educational Psychology* 98 (3): 529–41.

Chow, Ping-Ha, and Chi-Ting Chou. 2000. "Evaluating Sustained Silent Reading in Reading Classes." *The Internet TESL Journal* 6 (11).

Coiro, Julie, and Elizabeth Dobler. 2007. "Exploring the Online Reading Comprehension Strategies Used by Sixth Grade Skilled Readers to Search for and Locate Information on the Internet." *Reading Research Quarterly* 42: 214–57.

Coleman, David, and Sue Pimentel. 2012. "Revised Publisher's Criteria for the Common Core State Standards in English Language Arts and Literacy, Grades K–2." Available at: www.corestandards.org /assets/Publishers_Criteria_for_K-2.pdf. Accessed March 1, 2013.

Constantino, Rebecca. 2005. "Print Environments Between High and Low Socioeconomic Status (SES) Communities." *Teacher Librarian* 32 (3): 22.

Constantino, Rebecca, and Stephen Krashen. 2008. "It's Not Rocket Science: Students Know What Is Good for Them: The Efficacy of a Quality School Library." *Knowledge Quest* 36 4 (4): 60–63.

Daniels, Harvey. 2002. *Literature Circles: Voice and Choice in Book Clubs and Reading Groups.* Portland, ME: Stenhouse.

Donahue, Patricia L., R. J. Finnegan, Anthony D. Lutkus, Nancy L. Allen, and Jay R. Campbell. 2001. "The Nation's Report Card: Fourth-Grade Reading 2000." Washington, DC: U.S. Department of Education, Office of Educational Research and Improvement, National Center for Education Statistics.

Donovan, Carol A., Laura B. Smolkin, and Richard G. Lomax. 2000. "Beyond the Independent-Level Text: Considering the Reader-Text Match in First Graders' Self-Selections During Recreational Reading." *Reading Psychology* 21: 309–33.

Duke, Nell K. 2000a. "3.6 Minutes Per Day: The Scarcity of Informational Texts in First Grade." *Reading Research Quarterly* 35: 202–24.

———. 2000b. "For the Rich It's Richer: Print Experiences and Environments Offered to Children in Very Low- and Very High-Socioeconomic Status First-Grade Classrooms." *American Educational Research Journal* 37 (2): 441–78.

Duke, Nell K., and Kathryn L. Roberts. 2010. "The Genre-Specific Nature of Reading Comprehension." In *The Routledge International Handbook of English, Language and Literacy Teaching*, edited by Dominic Wyse, Richard Andrews, and James Hoffman, 74–86. London: Routledge.

Dynarski, Mark, Roberto Agodini, Shelia N. Heaviside, Nancy Carey, Larissa Campuzano, and Barbara Means. 2007. "Effectiveness of Reading and Mathematics Software Products: Findings from the First Student Cohort." Washington, DC: Institute for Education Sciences, U.S. Department of Education.

Ehri, Linnea C., Lois G. Dreyer, Bert Flugman, and Alan Gross. 2007. "Reading Rescue: An Effective Tutoring Intervention Model for Language-Minority Students Who Are Struggling Readers in First Grade." *American Educational Research Journal* 44 (2): 414–48.

Elley, Warwick B. 1992. "How in the World Do Students Read? The LEA Study of Reading Literacy." The Hague, Netherlands: International Association for the Evaluation of Educational Achievement.

Foertsch, Mary A. 1992. "Reading In and Out of School: Achievement of American Students in Grades 4, 8, and 12 in 1989–90." Washington, DC: National Center for Educational Statistics, U.S. Government Printing Office.

Foorman, Barbara R., Christopher Schatschneider, Michelle N. Eakin, Jack M. Fletcher, Louisa C. Moats, and David J. Francis. 2006. "The Impact of Instructional Practices in Grades 1 and 2 on Reading and Spelling Achievement in High Poverty Schools." *Contemporary Educational Psychology* 31: 1–29.

Fountas, I., and Gay Su Pinnell. 1996. *Guided Reading.* Portsmouth, NH: Heinemann.

———. 2001. *Guiding Readers and Writers: Grades 3–6: Teaching Comprehension, Genre and Content Literacy.* Portsmouth, NH: Heinemann.

Galleano, Eduardo. 1992. "Bureaucracy 3." In: *The Book of Embraces.* New York: W. W. Norton.

Gambrell, Linda B. 1984. "How Much Time Do Children Spend Reading During Teacher-Directed Reading Instruction?" In *Changing Perspectives on Research in Reading/Language Processing and Instruction.* Third Yearbook of the National Reading Conference, edited by Jerome A. Niles and Larry A. Harris, 193–98. Rochester, NY: National Reading Conference.

———. 1995. "Motivation Matters." In *Generations of Literacy, The Seventeenth Yearbook of the College Reading Association*, edited by W. M. Linek and E. G. Sturtevant, 2–24. Commerce, TX: College Reading Association.

Gambrell, Linda B., Barbara A. Marinak, Heather R. Brooker, and Heather J. McCrea-Andrews. 2011. "The Importance of Independent Reading." In *What Research Has to Say About Reading Instruction*, edited by S. J. Samuels and Alan E. Farstrup, 143–58. Newark, DE: International Reading Association.

Gamse, Beth C., Robin Tepper Jacob, Megan Horst, Beth Boulay, and Faith Unlu. 2008. "Reading First Impact Study Final Report." Washington, DC: National Center for Education Evaluation and Regional Assistance.

Garan, Elaine M., and Glenn DeVoogd. 2008. "The Benefits of Sustained Silent Reading: Scientific Research and Common Sense Converge." *The Reading Teacher* 62 (4): 336–44.

Guthrie, John T. 2004. "Teaching for Reading Engagement." *Journal of Literacy Research* 36: 1–28.

Guthrie, John T., Allan Wigfield, and Kathleen C. Perencevich. 2004. *Motivating Reading Comprehension: Concept-Oriented Reading Instruction*. Mahwah, NJ: Lawrence Erlbaum Associates.

Guthrie, John T., and Nicole M. Humenick. 2004. "Motivating Students to Read: Evidence for Classroom Practices That Increase Motivation and Achievement." In *The Voice of Evidence in Reading Research*, edited by Peggy McCardle and Vinita Chabra, 329–54. Baltimore, MD: Paul H. Brookes.

Guthrie, John T., William D. Schafer, and Chun-Wei Huang. 2001. "Benefits of Opportunity to Read and Balanced Instruction in the NAEP." *Journal of Educational Research* 94: 145–62.

Guthrie, John T., William D. Schafer, Clare Von Secker, and Terry Alban. 2000. "Contributions of Integrated Reading Instruction and Text Resources to Achievement and Engagement in a Statewide School Improvement Program." *Journal of Educational Research* 93: 211–26.

Hairrell, Angela, Meaghan Edmonds, Sharon Vaughn, and Deborah Simmons. 2010. "Independent Silent Reading for Struggling Readers: Pitfalls and Potential." In *Revisiting Silent Reading: New Directions for Teachers and Researchers*, edited by Elfreida H. Hiebert and D. Ray Reutzel, 275–89. Newark, DE: International Reading Association.

Halladay, Juliet. 2012. "Revisiting Key Assumptions of the Reading Level Framework." *The Reading Teacher* 66 (1): 53–62.

Hansen, Laurie E., Penny Collins, and Mark Warschauer. 2009. "Reading Management Programs: A Review of the Research." *Journal of Literacy and Technology* 10 (3): 55–80.

Hiebert, Elfreida H., and Charles W. Fisher. 2012. "Fluency from the First: What Works with First Graders." In *Fluency Instruction: Research-Based Best Practices*, edited by Timothy Rasinski, Camille L. Z. Blachowicz, and Kristin Lems, 279–92. New York: Guilford Press.

International Reading Association (IRA). 1999. "Providing Books and Other Print Materials for Classroom and School Libraries: A Position Statement of the International Reading Association." Newark, DE: International Reading Association.

Ivey, Gay, and Karen Broaddus. 2001. " 'Just Plain Reading': A Survey of What Makes Students Want to Read in Middle School Classrooms." *Reading Research Quarterly* 36: 350–77.

Jeong, Jongseong, Janet S. Gaffney, and Jin-Oh Choi. 2010. "Availability and Use of Informational Texts in Second-, Third- and Fourth-Grade Classrooms." *Research in the Teaching of English* 44 (4): 435–56.

Kamil, Michael L. 2008. *How to Get Recreational Reading to Increase Reading Achievement*. In *57th Yearbook of the National Reading Conference*, edited by Youb Kim et al., 31–40. Oak Creek, WI: National Reading Conference.

Kelly, Michelle, and Nicki Clausen-Grace. 2006. "The Sustained Silent Reading Makeover That Transformed Readers." *The Reading Teacher* 60 (2): 148–56.

Kim, James S. 2003. "Summer Reading and the Ethnic Achievement Gap." Paper presented at the American Educational Research Association, Chicago, April 23–25.

Kim, James S., and Jonathan Guryan. 2010. "The Efficacy of a Voluntary Summer Book Reading Intervention for Low-Income Latino Children from Language Minority Families." *Journal of Educational Psychology* 102 (1): 20–31.

Kim, James S., and Thomas G. White. 2008. "Scaffolding Voluntary Summer Reading for Children in Grades 3 to 5: An Experimental Study." Scientific Studies of Reading 12 (1): 1–23.

Kletzien, Sharon B., and Robert J. Szabo. 1998. "Information Text or Narrative Text? Children's Preferences Revisited." Paper presented at the National Reading Conference, Austin, TX.

Krashen, Stephen. 1995. "School Libraries, Public Libraries, and the NAEP Reading Scores." *School Library Media Quarterly* 23: 235–37.

———. 2011. *Free Voluntary Reading*. Santa Barbara, CA: Libraries Unlimited.

Krashen, Stephen, Syying Lee, and Jeff McQuillan. 2012. "Is the Library Important? Multivariate Studies at the National and International Level." *Journal of Language and Literacy Education (Online)* 8 (1): 26–38.

Kuhn, Melanie R. 2005. "A Comparative Study of Small Group Fluency Instruction." *Reading Psychology* 26 (2): 127–46.

Kuhn, Melanie. R., and Paula. J. Schwanenflugel. 2009. "Time, Engagement, and Support: Lessons from a 4-Year Fluency Intervention." In *Reading More, Reading Better*, edited by E. H. Hiebert, 141–60. New York: Guilford.

Kuhn, Melanie R., and Stephen A. Stahl. 2000. "Fluency: A Review of Developmental and Remedial Practices." Ann Arbor, MI: Center for the Improvement of Early Reading Achievement.

Lee, Jihyun, Wendy S. Grigg, and Patricia L. Donahue. 2007. "The Nation's Report Card: Reading 2007." Washington, DC: National Center for Education Statistics, Institute of Education Sciences, U.S. Department of Education.

Lewis, Marta. 2002. "Read More—Read Better? A Meta-Analysis of the Literature on the Relationship Between Exposure to Reading and Reading Achievement." Unpublished PhD diss., University of Minnesota.

Lewis, Marta, and S. J. Samuels. 2005. *Read More—Read Better? A Meta-Analysis of the Literature on the Relationship Between Exposure to Reading and Reading Achievement.* Minneapolis: University of Minnesota.

Lindsay, Jim. 2010. "Children's Access to Print Material and Education-Related Outcomes: Findings from a Meta-Analytic Review." Naperville, IL: Learning Point Associates.

Maloch, Beth. 2005. "Moments by Which Change Is Made: A Cross-Case Exploration of Teacher Mediation and Student Participation in Literacy Events." *Journal of Literacy Research* 37 (1): 95–142.

Manning, Gary L., and Mary Ann Manning. 1984. "What Models of Recreational Reading Make a Difference?" *Reading World* 42: 266–73.

Manning, Mary Ann, Marta Lewis, and Marsha Lewis. 2010. "Sustained Silent Reading: An Update of the Research." In *Revisiting Silent Reading: New Directions for Teachers and Researchers*, edited by E. H. Hiebert and D. R. Reutzel, 112–27. Newark, DE: International Reading Association.

Marshall, Jodi C. 2002. *Are They Really Reading? Expanding SSR in the Middle Grades.* Portland, ME: Stenhouse.

Martinez, Miriam, Nancy L. Roser, Jo Worthy, Susan Strecker, and Philip Gough. 1997. "Classroom Libraries and Children's Book Selections: Redefining 'Access' in Self-Selected Reading." In *Inquiries in Literacy Theory and Practice: 46th Yearbook of the National Reading Conference*, edited by C. K. Kinzer, K. A. Hinchman, and D. J. Leu, 265–72. Chicago, IL: National Reading Conference.

McGroarty, John Joseph. 1982. "The Effect of Varied Amounts of Sustained Silent Reading (SSR) on Selected Aspects of Reading/Thinking Skills and Attitude Toward Reading." PhD diss., Temple University, Philadelphia, PA.

McIntyre, Ellen, Diane W. Kyle, and Gayle H. Moore. 2006. "A Primary Grade Teacher's Guidance Toward Small-Group Dialogue." *Reading Research Quarterly* 41 (1): 36–66.

McIntyre, Ellen, Elizabeth Rightmyer, Rebecca Powell, Sherry Powers, and Joseph Petrosko. 2006. "How Much Should Young Children Read? A Study of the Relationship Between Development and Instruction." *Literacy Teaching and Learning* 11 (1): 51–72.

McMahon, Susan I., and Virginia J. Goatley. 1995. "Fifth Graders Helping Peers Discuss Texts in Student-Led Groups." *Journal of Educational Research* 89 (1): 23–34.

McQuillan, J. 1998. *The Literacy Crisis: False Claims and Real Solutions.* Portsmouth, NH: Heinemann.

Methe, Scott A., and John M. Hinze. 2003. "Evaluating Teacher Modeling as a Strategy to Increase Student Reading Behavior." *School Psychology Review* 32 (4): 617–23.

Miller, Debbie. 2013. *Reading with Meaning: Teaching Comprehension in the Primary Grades.* 2d ed. Portland, ME: Stenhouse.

Morrow, Lesley M. 2003. "Motivating Lifelong Voluntary Readers." In *Handbook of Research on Teaching the English Language Arts*, edited by James Flood, Diane Lapp, James R. Squire, and Julie M. Jensen, 857–67. Mahwah, NJ: Lawrence Erlbaum Associates.

Moss, Barbara. 2003. *Exploring the Literature of Fact: Children's Nonfiction Trade Books in the Elementary Classroom.* New York: Guilford.

———. 2008. "The Information Text Gap: The Mismatch Between Non-Narrative Text Types in Basal Readers and 2009 NAEP Recommended Guidelines." *Journal of Literacy Research* 40: 201–219.

Mullis, Ina V. S., Michael O. Martin, Ann M. Kennedy, and Pierre Foy. 2007. "PIRLS 2006 International Report." Boston University: International Study Center.

Murphy, P. Karen, Anna O. Soter, Ian A. G. Wilkinson, Maeghan N. Hennessey, and Jon F. Alexander. 2009. "Examining the Effects of Classroom Discussion on Students' Comprehension of Texts: A Meta-Analysis." *Journal of Educational Psychology* 101 (3): 740–64.

National Center for Education Statistics, Institute of Education Sciences, U.S. Department of Education. 2009. *The Nation's Report Card: Reading 2009.* Washington, DC: National Center for Education Statistics, Institute of Education Sciences, U.S. Department of Education.

———. 2011. *The Nation's Report Card: Reading 2011* (NCES 2012–457). Washington, DC: National Center for Education Statistics, Institute of Education Sciences, U.S. Department of Education.

National Endowment for the Arts. 2007. "To Read or Not to Read: A Question of National Consequence." Washington, DC: National Endowment for the Arts.

National Governors Association Center for Best Practices, Council of Chief State School Officers. 2010. Common Core State Standards in English Language Arts and Literacy in History/Social Studies Science and Technical Subjects. Washington, DC: National Governors Association Center for Best Practices, Council of Chief State School Officers.

National Institute of Child Health and Human Development (NICHHD). 2000. *Report of the National Reading Panel: Teaching Children to Read: An Evidence-Based Assessment of the Scientific Research Literature on Reading and Its Implications for Reading Instruction.* Washington, DC: National Institute of Child Health and Human Development.

Ness, Molly. 2011. "Teachers' Use of and Attitudes Toward Informational Text in K–5 Classrooms." *Reading Psychology* 32 (1): 28–53.

Neuman, Susan B. 1999. "Books Make a Difference: A Study of Access to Literacy." *Reading Research Quarterly* 34: 286–311.

Neuman, Susan B., and Donna Celano. 2001. "Access to Print in Low-Income and Middle-Income Communities." *Reading Research Quarterly* 36 (1): 8–26.

Newman, Terry H. 2007. Factors That Motivate Fifth Grade Students to Read During Sustained Silent Reading (SSR). PhD diss., University of Maryland.

Nystrand, Martin. 2006. "Research on the Role of Classroom Discourse as It Affects Reading Comprehension." *Research in the Teaching of English* 40 (4): 392–412.

O'Conner, Rollanda E., Kathryn M. Bell, Kristin Harty, Louise K. Larkin, Sharry M. Sackor, and Naomi Zigmond. 2002. "Teaching Reading to Poor Readers in Intermediate Grades: A Comparison of Text Difficulty." *Journal of Educational Psychology* 94: 474–85.

Oczkus, Lori. 2010. *Reciprocal Teaching at Work K–12*, 2d ed. Newark, DE: International Reading Association.

Palincsar, Annemarie S., and Ann L. Brown. 1984. "Reciprocal Teaching of Comprehension-Fostering and Comprehension-Monitoring Activities." *Cognition and Instruction* 1 (2): 117–75.

Palincsar, Annemarie S., and Nell K. Duke. 2004. "The Role of Text and Text-Reader Interactions in Young Children's Reading Development and Achievement." *The Elementary School Journal* 105 (2): 183–97.

Reis, Sally M., Rebecca D. Eckert, D. Betsy McCoach, Joan K. Jacobs, and Michael Coyne. 2008. "Using Enrichment Reading Practices to Increase Reading Fluency, Comprehension and Attitudes." *The Journal of Educational Research* 101 (5): 299–315.

Reutzel, D. Ray, Cindy D. Jones, Parker C. Fawson, and John A. Smith. 2008. "Scaffolded Silent Reading: A Complement to Guided Repeated Oral Reading That Works!" *The Reading Teacher* 62 (3): 194–207.

Reutzel, D. Ray, Cindy D. Jones, and Terry H. Newman. 2010. "Scaffolded Silent Reading: Improving the Conditions of Silent Reading Practice." In *Revisiting Silent Reading: New Directions for Teachers and Researchers*, edited by Elfreida H. Hiebert and D. Ray Reutzel, 129–50. Newark, DE: International Reading Association.

Reutzel, D. Ray, Parker C. Fawson, and John A. Smith. 2008. "Reconsidering Silent Sustained Reading: An Exploratory Study of Scaffolded Silent Reading." *Journal of Educational Research* 102 (1): 37–50.

Reynolds, P. Lee, and Sonya Symons. 2001. "Motivational Variables and Children's Text Search." *Journal of Educational Psychology* 93: 14–22.

Sanden, Sherry. 2012. "Independent Reading: Perspectives and Practices of Highly Effective Teachers." *Reading Teacher* 66 (3): 222–31.

Saunders, William M., and Claude Goldenberg. 1999. "Effects of Instructional Conversations and Literature Logs on Limited- and Fluent-English-Proficient Students' Story Comprehension and Thematic Understanding." *Elementary School Journal* 99: 277–301.

Savage, Stephen. 2006. *Rainforest Animals* (*Focus on Habitats*). London: Hodder Wayland Childrens.

Sinclair-Tarr, Stacy, and William Tarr. 2007. "Using Large Scale Assessments to Evaluate the Effectiveness of School Library Programs in California." *Phi Delta Kappan* 88: 710–12.

Soter, Anna O., Ian A. Wilkinson, P. Karen Murphy, Lucila Ludge, Kristin Reninger, and Margaret Edwards. 2008. "What the Discourse Tells Us: Talk and Indicators of High-Level Comprehension." *International Journal of Educational Research* 48 (1): 740–64.

Soter, Anna O., and Lucila Rudge. 2005. "What the Discourse Tells Us: Talk and Indicators of High-Level Comprehension." Paper presented at conference for the American Educational Research Association. Montreal, Ontario, Canada.

Stahl, Steven A., and Kathleen M. Heuback. 2005. "Fluency-Oriented Reading Instruction." *Journal of Literacy Research* 36: 25–60.

Taylor, Barbara M., Barbara J. Frye, and Geoffrey M. Maruyama. 1990. "Time Spent Reading and Reading Growth." *American Educational Research Journal* 27: 351–62.

Taylor, Barbara M., P. David Pearson, Debra S. Peterson, and Michael C. Rodriguez. 2003. "Reading Growth in High-Poverty Classrooms: The Influence of Teacher Practices That Encourage Cognitive Engagement in Literacy Learning." *Elementary School Journal* 104 (1): 3–28.

Topping, Keith J., S. Jay Samuels, and T. Paul. 2007. "Does Practice Make Perfect? Independent Reading Quantity, Quality and Student Achievement." *Learning and Instruction* 17 (3): 253–64.

Torgensen, Joseph K., and Roxanne F. Hudson. 2006. "Reading Fluency: Critical Issues for Struggling Readers." In *Reading Fluency: The Forgotten Dimension of Reading Success*, edited by S. J. Samuels and A. Farstrup, 13–158. Newark, DE: International Reading Association.

Trudel, Heidi. 2007. "Making Data-Driven Decisions: Silent Reading." *The Reading Teacher* 61 (40): 308–15.

White, Thomas G., and James S. Kim. 2010. "Can Silent Reading in the Summer Reduce Socioeconomic Differences in Reading Achievement?" In *Revisiting Silent Reading: New Directions for Teachers and Researchers*, edited by E. H. Hiebert and D. Ray Reutzel, 67–91. Newark, DE: International Reading Association.

Widdowson, Deborah A. M., Robyn S. Dixon, and Dennis W. Moore. 2006. "The Effects of Teacher Modeling of Silent Reading on Students' Engagement During Sustained Silent Reading." *Educational Psychology: An International Journal of Experimental Educational Psychology* 16 (2): 171–80.

Worthy, Jo, Megan Moorman, and Margo Turner. 1999. "What Johnny Likes to Read Is Hard to Find in School." *Reading Research Quarterly* 34: 12–27.

Wu, Yi-Chen, and S. Jay Samuels. 2004. "How the Amount of Time Spent on Independent Reading Affects Reading Achievement: A Response to the National Reading Panel." Paper presented at The International Reading Association 49th Annual Convention, Reno, Nevada.

Yopp, Ruth Helen, and Hallie Kay Yopp. 2006. "Informational Texts as Read-Alouds at School and Home." *Journal of Literacy Research* 38 (1): 37–51.

Children's Literature Cited

Burnett, Frances Hodgson. 2005. *The Secret Garden*. New York: Sterling Publishing.

Carmi, Giora. 2003. *A Circle of Friends*. New York: Star Bright Books.

Cole, Henry. 2012. *Unspoken*. New York: Scholastic.

DiCamillo, Kate. 2010. *Because of Winn-Dixie*. Somerville, MA: Candlewick.

Guthrie, Woody. 2010. *This Land Is Your Land*. Illus. Kathy Jakobsen. Boston: Little, Brown Books for Young Readers.

Lobel, Arnold. 1970–1979. Frog and Toad series. New York: HarperCollins.

Martin, Bill Jr. 1967. *Brown Bear, Brown Bear, What Do You See?* New York: Holt, Rinehart, and Winston.

McPhail, David. 2009. *No!* New York: Roaring Brook Press.

Pinkney, Jerry. 2009. *The Lion and the Mouse*. New York: Little, Brown.

Tallec, Oliver. 2012. *Trafalgar and Waterloo*. New York: Enchanted Lion Books.

Tan, Shaun. 2006. *The Arrival*. New York: Scholastic.

Westcott, Nadine Bernard. 1998. *The Lady with the Alligator Purse*. Boston: Little, Brown.

White, E. B. 2006. *Charlotte's Web*. New York: HarperCollins.

Winter, Jeanette. 2009. *Nasreen's Secret School: A True Story from Afghanistan*. New York: Beach Lane Books/Simon & Schuster.